The incredible Ripley's team has stalked through graveyards all over the world to bring you this amazing collection of facts, rituals, and events surrounding **Tombstones and Graveyards!**

If you cannot find your favorite ***Believe It or Not!*** POCKET BOOK at your local newsstand, please write to the nearest Ripley's "Believe It or Not!" museum:

175 Jefferson Street, San Francisco,
California 94133

1500 North Wells Street, Chicago,
Illinois 60610

19 San Marco Avenue, St. Augustine,
Florida 32084

The Parkway
Gatlinburg, Tennessee 37738

145 East Elkhorn Avenue, Estes Park,
Colorado 80517

4960 Clifton Hill, Niagara Falls,
Canada

Central Promenade, Blackpool,
Lancashire, England

Ripley's Believe It or Not! titles

Ripley's Believe It or Not! 2nd Series
Ripley's Believe It or Not! 3rd Series
Ripley's Believe It or Not! 4th Series
Ripley's Believe It or Not! 5th Series
Ripley's Believe It or Not! 6th Series
Ripley's Believe It or Not! 7th Series
Ripley's Believe It or Not! 8th Series
Ripley's Believe It or Not! 9th Series
Ripley's Believe It or Not! 10th Series
Ripley's Believe It or Not! 11th Series
Ripley's Believe It or Not! 12th Series
Ripley's Believe It or Not! 13th Series
Ripley's Believe It or Not! 14th Series
Ripley's Believe It or Not! 15th Series
Ripley's Believe It or Not! 16th Series
Ripley's Believe It or Not! 17th Series
Ripley's Believe It or Not! 18th Series
Ripley's Believe It or Not! 19th Series
Ripley's Believe It or Not! 20th Series
Ripley's Believe It or Not! 21st Series
Ripley's Believe It or Not! 22nd Series
Ripley's Believe It or Not! 23rd Series
Ripley's Believe It or Not! 24th Series
Ripley's Believe It or Not! 25th Series
Ripley's Believe It or Not! 26th Series
Ripley's Believe It or Not! Anniversary Edition
Ripley's Believe It or Not! Book of Americana
Ripley's Believe It or Not! Book of the Military
Ripley's Believe It or Not! Book of Undersea Oddities
Ripley's Believe It or Not! Tombstones and Graveyards

Published by POCKET BOOKS

Ripley's Believe It or Not!

TOMBSTONES AND GRAVEYARDS

A KANGAROO BOOK
PUBLISHED BY POCKET BOOKS NEW YORK

RIPLEY'S BELIEVE IT OR NOT!®
TOMBSTONES AND GRAVEYARDS

POCKET BOOK edition published 1966

This original POCKET BOOK edition is printed from brand-new plates made from newly set, clear, easy-to-read type.
POCKET BOOK editions are published by
POCKET BOOKS,
a Simon & Schuster Division of
GULF & WESTERN CORPORATION
1230 Avenue of the Americas,
New York, N.Y. 10020.
Trademarks registered in the United States and other countries.

2387

ISBN: 0-671-81463-X.

Printed in the U.S.A.

THE STRANGE SENTINELS OF SUMATRA
Indonesia

WATCHMEN CARVED FROM WOOD -*COMPLETE WITH A GUN FOR PROTECTION AND A BLANKET FOR WARMTH*- GUARD THE GRAVES OF THE CHIEFS OF THE KARO BATAK TRIBE

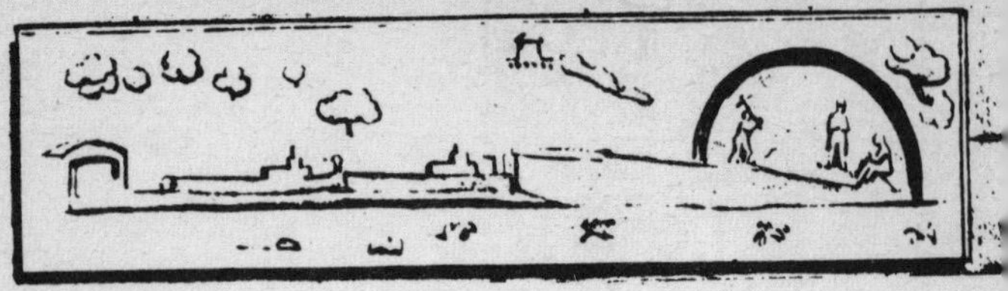

THE TOMBSTONE OF JOSEPH PRIESTLEY, WHO BUILT THE LEEDS AND LIVERPOOL CANAL IN ENGLAND, *IS A REPLICA OF PART OF THAT CANAL* — Bradford, England

INSCRIPTION ON TOMBSTONE -
MORAVIAN CEMETERY — New Dorp, Staten Is. N.Y.

EVERGREEN CEMETERY, Paris, Texas

The TOMB of the MISSING
Ouessant Island, France,
A MINIATURE CHAPEL IN THE LOCAL CEMETERY IN WHICH A CROSS IS BURIED EACH TIME AN INHABITANT OF THE ISLAND *DIES IN A DISTANT LAND OR IS LOST AT SEA*

GHOST

GHOST IN A CEMETERY
Grove City, Pa

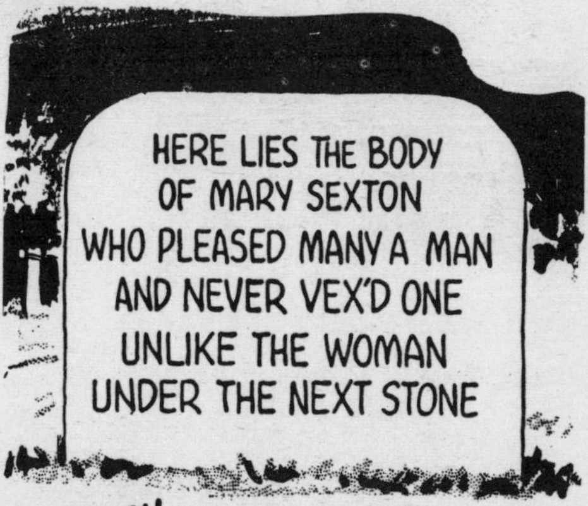
HERE LIES THE BODY
OF MARY SEXTON
WHO PLEASED MANY A MAN
AND NEVER VEX'D ONE
UNLIKE THE WOMAN
UNDER THE NEXT STONE

EPITAPH in St. Mary's Churchyard
Bideford, England

THE MAN WHO WAS BURIED ALIVE
IBN SAFVI
a holy man of Beni Isguen, Algeria
SPENT 32 YEARS ENTOMBED IN A CONCRETE WALL – DEPENDENT FOR FOOD AND WATER ON PASSERSBY!
WHEN HE DIED HIS LIVING TOMB BECAME HIS BURIAL VAULT

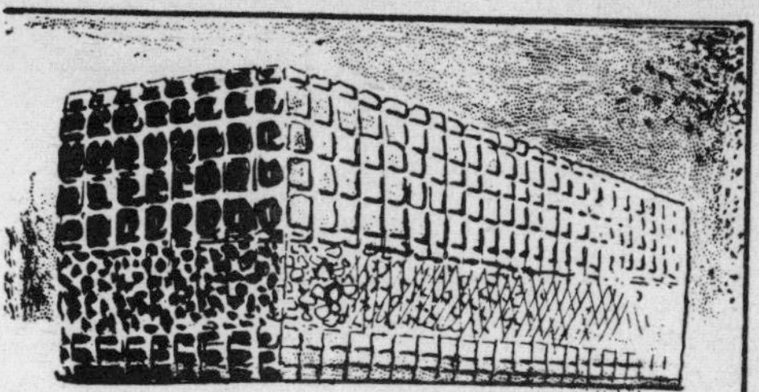

A **COFFIN**, FOUND IN Massarah, Egypt, in 1888 WAS MADE FROM THE ENTIRE HIDE OF A CROCODILE

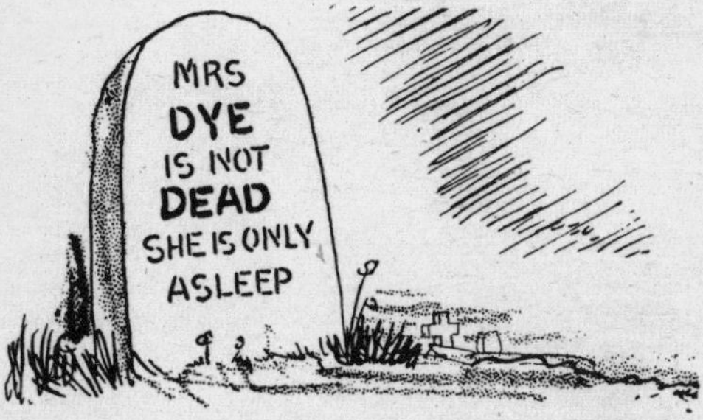
MRS
DYE
IS NOT
DEAD
SHE IS ONLY
ASLEEP

GRAVESTONE IN COONEWAH CREEK CEMETERY
Mississippi

P.S.
THE
OLD
NUISANCE

EPITAPH ON THE GRAVESTONE OF PHILIP SYDNEY, WHO HAD OVERHEARD MEMBERS OF HIS FAMILY DISCUSSING "*HOW MUCH LONGER THE OLD NUISANCE WOULD BE AROUND*"
East Calais, Vt.

THE MAN WHO HAS 10,000 TOMBSTONES!
KANG TANG
(921-957)
WHO GAVE HIS LIFE TO SAVE EMPEROR KUO JUNG FROM ASSASSINATION HAS A GRAVESTONE IN EVERY VILLAGE IN CHINA!
THE MONUMENTS BEARING KANG'S NAME ARE BELIEVED TO HAVE THE POWER TO WARD OFF ALL EVIL

THE **GRAVE** OF A POTTER in Tunisia IS ADORNED BY A LARGE POT *A SAMPLE OF HIS BEST WORK*

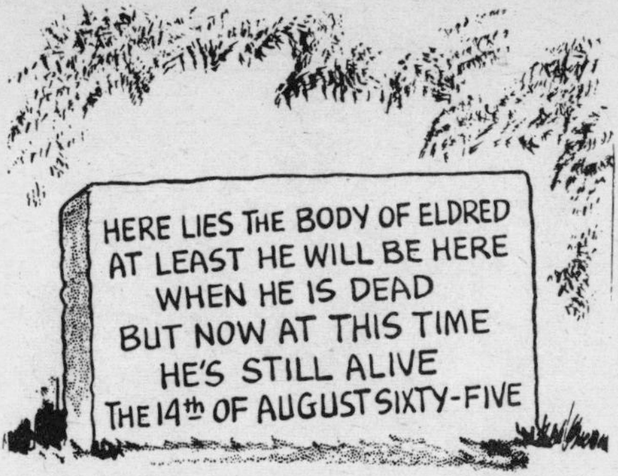
HERE LIES THE BODY OF ELDRED
AT LEAST HE WILL BE HERE
WHEN HE IS DEAD
BUT NOW AT THIS TIME
HE'S STILL ALIVE
THE 14th OF AUGUST SIXTY-FIVE

EPITAPH IN OXFORD CEMETERY England

Here Rests
SAMUEL WELLS
Born 1824-Died -
THE VICTIM OF A
DISHONEST WOMAN
NEVER HAD A CHILD OF HIS OWN
BUT
LOVED OTHER PEOPLES
LITTLE ONES

IN ROUND GROVE CEMETERY, Ill.

THE TOMB in Salona, Yugoslavia, OF MONSIGNOR FRANC BULIC, A CELEBRATED ARCHEOLOGIST, IS THE REPLICA OF AN ANCIENT ROMAN DWELLING AND BEARS THIS EPITAPH HE WROTE HIMSELF: ***"Here lies a sinner"***

THE MAN WHO REFUSED TO MOVE FROM HIS GRAVE
GAME SHAH of Rohtak. India
PICKED HIS BURIAL SITE AND THEN SAT UPON IT UNTIL HIS DEATH
-A PERIOD OF 37 YEARS!

THE GRAVE OF THE
FAITHFUL WIFE
The
STRANGEST PASSPORTS
TO HEAVEN ARE
WATER BUCKETS
ON THE GRAVES OF
AINU HOUSEWIVES!
-BEARING WITNESS
THAT SHE HAS FAITHFULLY
DISCHARGED HER WIFELY
DUTIES AND CHORES
ALL DURING
HER LIFETIME

HE GOT A FISHBONE
IN HIS THROAT
AND THEN HE SANG
AN ANGEL NOTE

EPITAPH
Schenectady, N.Y.

THE TOMB OF EARS IN KYOTO, JAPAN
DURING THE JAPANESE-KOREAN WAR - 1592/8
30,000 KOREANS WERE KILLED IN A
BATTLE AND THEIR EARS WERE
CUT OFF AS SYMBOLS OF VICTORY
AND CARRIED TO JAPAN WHERE
THEY WERE BURIED IN A HUGE
MOUND - THE "MIMIDSUKA"

EDWARD CAPERN
THE POSTMAN POET
BORN AT TIVERTON 21 JAN. 1819
DIED AT BRAUNTON 4 JUNE 1894

"TINKLING TOMBSTONE" —Heanton, Eng.

A RURAL POSTMAN'S BELL WAS PLACED ON HIS TOMBSTONE AND THE SLIGHTEST BREEZE CAUSES IT TO TINKLE!

HERE IS
A. GRAVE

ODD FELLOWS CEMETERY
Weimar, Texas

WAR EAGLE

Chief of the Yankton Sioux Indians
WAS BURIED IN SIOUX CITY, Iowa, ASTRIDE HIS HORSE AND WITH HIS EYES JUST ABOVE THE SURFACE OF THE GROUND
SO HE COULD CONTINUE TO OVERLOOK HIS OLD HUNTING GROUNDS

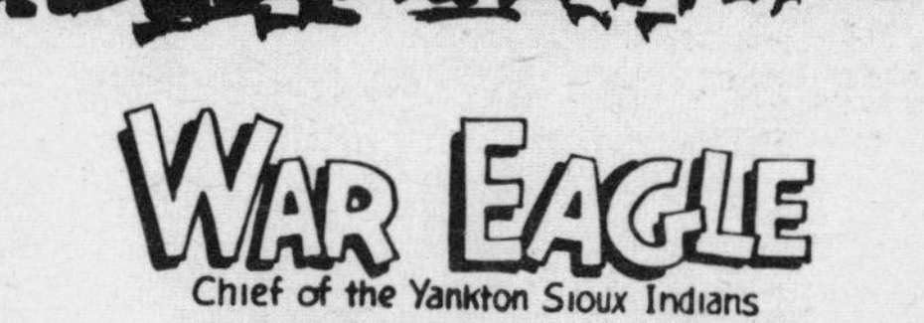
SACRED TO THE MEMORY OF
JARED BATES
WHO DIED AUG. 6, 1800
HIS WIDOW AGED 24 LIVES AT
7 ELM STREET AND POSSESSES EVERY
QUALIFICATION FOR A GOOD WIFE

Epitaph in Lincoln, Me.

TOMBSTONES SHAPED LIKE SHIPS USED IN BORNEO TO TRANSPORT THE SOUL TO HEAVEN

AMI
DEVINE

GRAVESTONE IN HAMPTON, Va.

MEANT WELL
TRIED A LITTLE
FAILED MUCH

TOMBSTONE IN Lakewood, N.J

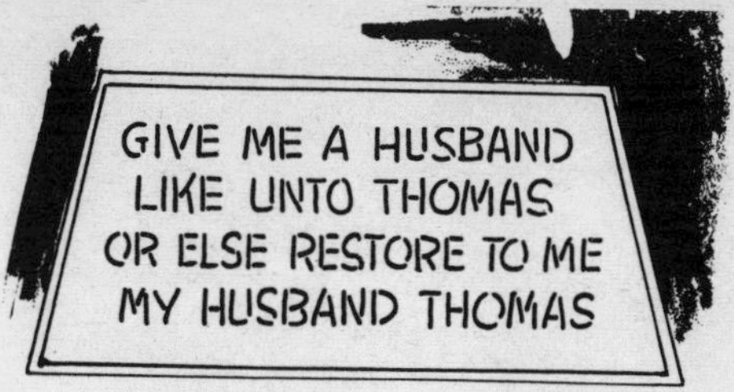
GIVE ME A HUSBAND
LIKE UNTO THOMAS
OR ELSE RESTORE TO ME
MY HUSBAND THOMAS

PROPHETIC EPITAPH
in Bisham Church, England,
PLACED OVER THE GRAVE OF SIR THOMAS HOBY BY HIS WIDOW, WHOSE PRAYER WAS ANSWERED WHEN SIR **THOMAS** RUSSELL BECAME HER SECOND HUSBAND

GHOST
TUNNELL

GRAVESTONE
in Woodlawn Cemetery
Edwardsville, Ill.

TOMB of SANTA CLAUS

In the Crypt of San Nicola, BARI, Italy

SANTA CLAUS REALLY LIVED AND HIS BODY IS BURIED IN THE CATHEDRAL OF ST. NICHOLAS, Bari

St Nick is not only the Patron Saint of Children But of Thieves and Pawnbrokers as Well!

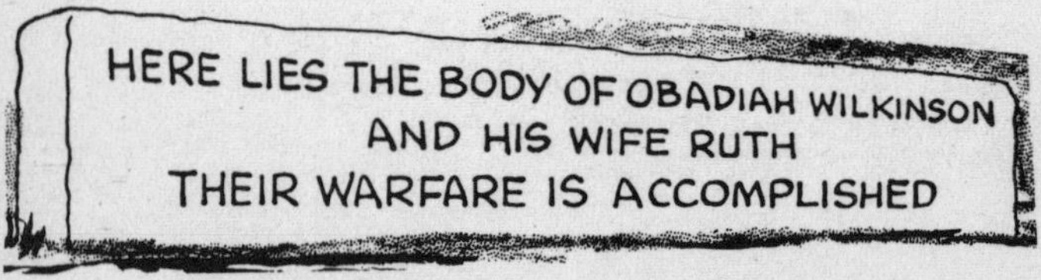
HERE LIES THE BODY OF OBADIAH WILKINSON
AND HIS WIFE RUTH
THEIR WARFARE IS ACCOMPLISHED

EPITAPH in Prescott, Mass.

A
KING
of the
Nyamwezi Tribe,
Africa
MUST
SPEND
8
DAYS
AND
NIGHTS
LOCKED
IN
THE
TOMB
OF
HIS
PREDECESSOR!

THE **CHURCH OF LE PLANÈS**
in France
ORIGINALLY WAS CONSTRUCTED AS THE TOMB OF AN ARAB REBEL NAMED MUNAZA WHO WAS EXECUTED DURING A MOORISH INVASION OF FRANCE IN 721

SOLDIER'S GRAVE
Montparnasse, Paris, Fr.

THE DOLL HOUSE MEMORIAL

A CHILD'S TOY KEPT IN PERFECT CONDITION FOR 66 YEARS!

OVER THE GRAVE OF A 12-YEAR-OLD CHILD —

Congregational Church Cemetery, Warren Township, N.J.

THE "BYDEING TYME" GRAVE Middlesex, Eng

WILLIAM AND AGNES LOUDON WERE BURIED ABOVE GROUND TO CIRCUMVENT THEIR RELATIVES FROM INHERITING THEIR PROPERTY.

THEY BELIEVED THAT "NOBODY CAN TOUCH A MAN'S PROPERTY UNTIL HE IS UNDER THE GROUND"

COFFIN DRUM of the AMAZON OCAINOS
LOG HOLLOWED OUT IN HUMAN FORM IS USED BY THE CHIEF AS A DRUM IN TIME OF WAR AND AS A COFFIN WHEN HE DIES

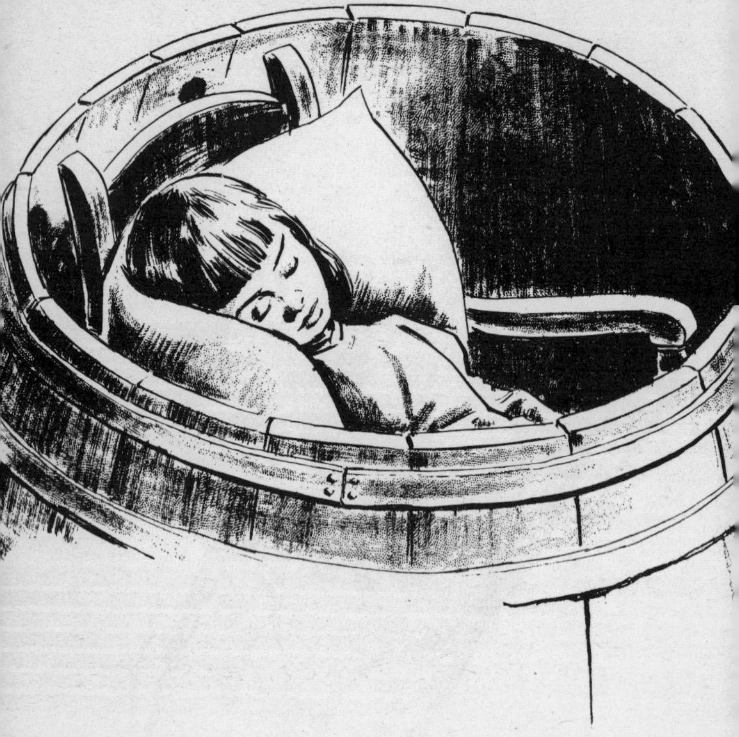

NANCY ADAMS MARTIN

A CHILD from Wilmington, N.C.
WHO DIED SEATED ON A CHAIR ON HER FATHER'S SHIP AT SEA, WAS BURIED STILL SEATED ON THE CHAIR, WITH A ***WOODEN CASK AS HER COFFIN***

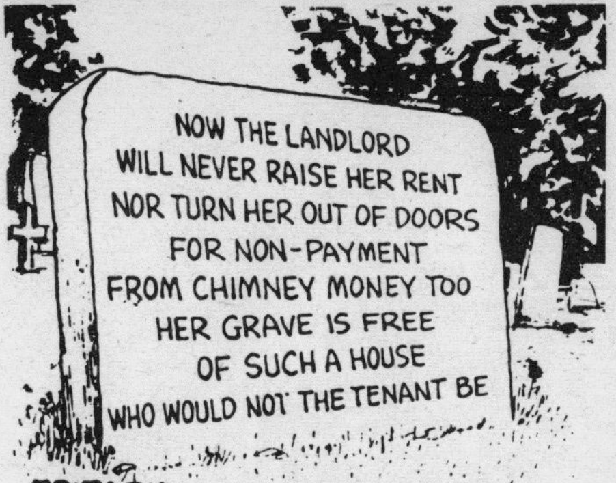
NOW THE LANDLORD
WILL NEVER RAISE HER RENT
NOR TURN HER OUT OF DOORS
FOR NON-PAYMENT
FROM CHIMNEY MONEY TOO
HER GRAVE IS FREE
OF SUCH A HOUSE
WHO WOULD NOT THE TENANT BE

EPITAPH OF REBECCA ROGERS
Folkestone Churchyard, England

STAY IN YOUR CAR

A **WARNING** TO MOTORISTS
TO BEWARE OF LIONS
at Serengeti Wildlife Park,
in Tanganyika, Africa,
FEATURES THE SKULL
AND CROSSED BONES
OF A LION

THE GRAVES OF WEALTHY CHINESE ARE EQUIPPED WITH **EARS**-- SO THE DEPARTED SOULS CAN KEEP WELL INFORMED!

*A SERVANT WHISPERS DAILY INTO THE MARBLE EARS THE **LATEST GOSSIP***

The SPRINGBOK
ON THE GRAVESTONE OF
KING SEKGOMA
of Bamanguato, S. Africa
EXPRESSES THE
KING'S HOPE TO BE
REINCARNATED AS
THIS ANIMAL

SOME MUST DIE THAT
OTHERS MAY LIVE
SAITH THE
GRAVEDIGGER

EPITAPH ON THE GRAVE OF POLLY LOVE in Dudley, Mass.

THE TOMB IN WHICH 8,000 MEN WERE BURIED ALIVE!

HUANG TI

FIRST CHINESE EMPEROR
WAS BURIED WITH SO VAST A TREASURE THAT
EVERY LABORER WHO HELPED BUILD HIS TOMB
WAS SEALED WITHIN ITS WALLS!

209 B.C.

HERE LIES
LOTTA
DUST

GRAVESTONE
IN ROSE LAWN CEMETERY
Detroit, Mich.

HE DIED
FOR THE
LOVE OF

TOMBSTONE IN GREENLAWN Cemetery
Portsmouth, Ohio

COPY
ALL IN

GRAVESTONE OF
FUZZY WOODRUFF, WELL KNOWN
GEORGIA JOURNALIST-Atlanta Cemetery

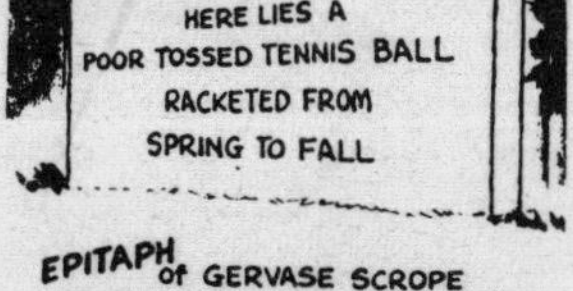
HERE LIES A
POOR TOSSED TENNIS BALL
RACKETED FROM
SPRING TO FALL

EPITAPH of GERVASE SCROPE
A TENNIS PLAYER WHO DIED OF GOUT
St. Mary's Hall, Coventry, England

THE GRAVE in Wilmot, N.H., OF A BUCKSKIN HORSE NAMED "BROWNIE" WHICH PULLED A CHUCKWAGON IN THE CIVIL WAR IS STILL DECORATED WITH AN AMERICAN FLAG EACH MEMORIAL DAY

THE GRAVESTONES THAT MARK NO GRAVES

THE MARINE CEMETERY of Narbonne, France, CONTAINS ONLY MEMORIALS TO NATIVE FISHERMEN AND SAILORS *WHOSE BODIES HAVE NEVER BEEN FOUND*

HERE LIES THE REMAINS
OF JAMES PADY . BRICKMAKER,
IN THE HOPE THAT HIS CLAY
WILL BE REMOULDED IN A
WORKMANLIKE MANNER.
FAR SUPERIOR TO HIS
FORMER PERISHABLE
MATERIALS

EPITAPH in Addiscombe Churchyard
Devonshire, England

EPITAPH ON THE
GRAVE OF AN
UNKNOWN SAILOR
in Patrick Churchyard,
Isle of Man

SOME
MOTHER'S
SON

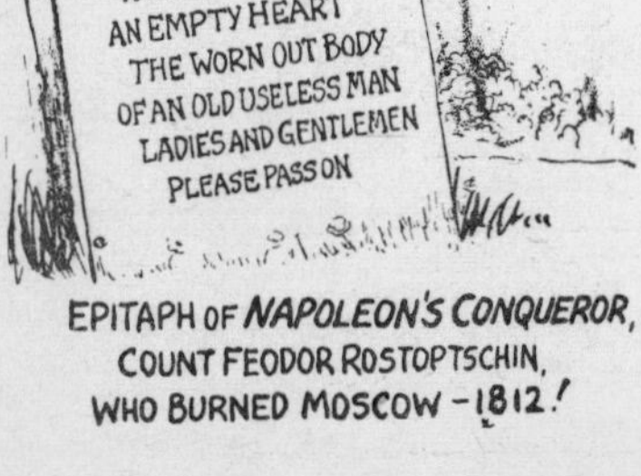
HERE LIES FOREVER
A WOUNDED SOUL,
AN EMPTY HEART
THE WORN OUT BODY
OF AN OLD USELESS MAN
LADIES AND GENTLEMEN
PLEASE PASS ON

EPITAPH OF *NAPOLEON'S CONQUEROR*,
COUNT FEODOR ROSTOPTSCHIN,
WHO BURNED MOSCOW – 1812!

THE GRAVE OF THE LIVING
Goyaz, Brazil

A BRIEF REST IN THIS TOMB IS BELIEVED TO ASSURE GOOD HEALTH-- *BECAUSE* ***3** PERSONS BURIED IN IT* ***RETURNED TO LIFE!***

AN ORNATE TOMB
near Imerina, Madagascar,
IS PROVIDED WITH A CLOCK WHICH IS WOUND REGULARLY BY THE DECEASED'S FAMILY *SO HE WILL BE ABLE TO KEEP TRACK OF THE PASSING HOURS*

KING
SOLOMON

IS BURIED IN
LEXINGTON, Kentucky

Beneath this tree
lie singers three
One tenor and two bases
Now they're gone its 10-1
If three will take their places

EPITAPH in Forden, Wales

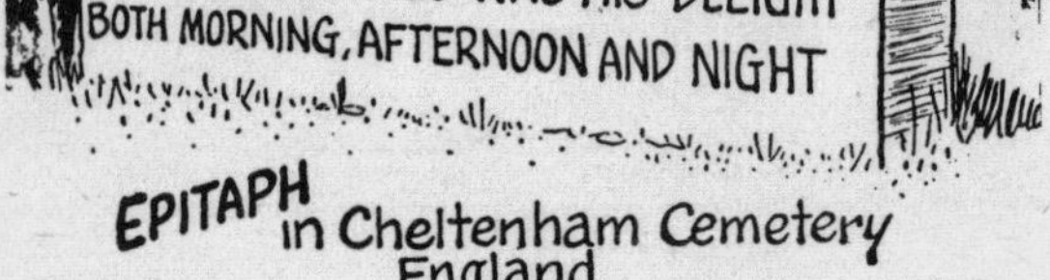
HERE LIES JOHN HIGGS
A FAMOUS MAN FOR KILLING PIGS
FOR KILLING PIGS WAS HIS DELIGHT
BOTH MORNING, AFTERNOON AND NIGHT

EPITAPH in Cheltenham Cemetery
England

GRAVESTONE
OF A WOMAN WHO
DIED FROM THE EFFECTS
OF *TIGHT LACING*
Springkell, Scotland

THE ANAGRAM OF
FUNERAL IS **REAL FUN**

LIE HEAVY ON HIM EARTH!
FOR HE
LAID MANY HEAVY LOADS
ON THEE

EPITAPH
ON THE GRAVE
OF AN ARCHITECT
St. Stephen's Churchyard
London

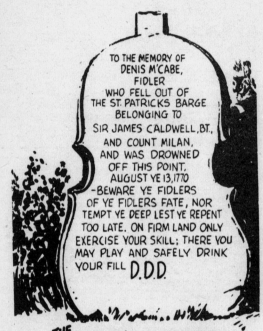

TO THE MEMORY OF
DENIS M'CABE,
FIDLER
WHO FELL OUT OF
THE ST. PATRICKS BARGE
BELONGING TO
SIR JAMES CALDWELL, BT.,
AND COUNT MILAN,
AND WAS DROWNED
OFF THIS POINT,
AUGUST YE 13, 1770
-BEWARE YE FIDLERS
OF YE FIDLERS FATE, NOR
TEMPT YE DEEP LEST YE REPENT
TOO LATE. ON FIRM LAND ONLY
EXERCISE YOUR SKILL; THERE YOU
MAY PLAY AND SAFELY DRINK
YOUR FILL D.D.D.

THE FIDDLER'S TOMBSTONE

Castlecaldwell, Lough Ern, Ireland

ERECTED IN MEMORY OF DENIS McCABE, Fidler
WITH THIS INSCRIPTION
"D.D.D." Meaning "DENIS DIED DRUNK"

HERE LIE THE REMAINS OF JOHN HALL
GROCER
THE WORLD IS NOT WORTH A FIG
I HAVE GOOD RAISINS FOR SAYING SO

EPITAPH IN DUNMORE CEMETERY
Ireland

GOD'S ANGEL BAND WAS NOT COMPLETE TILL KATIE WENT AND TOOK HER SEAT

EPITAPH IN
ZION LUTHERAN CEMETERY
New Palestine, Ind.

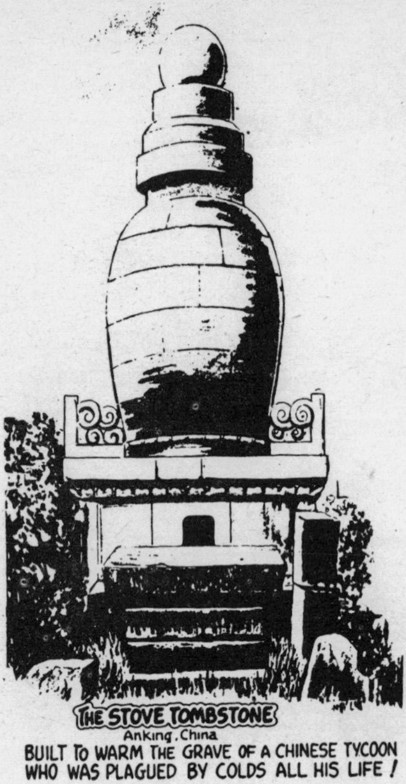

THE STOVE TOMBSTONE
Anking, China
BUILT TO WARM THE GRAVE OF A CHINESE TYCOON WHO WAS PLAGUED BY COLDS ALL HIS LIFE!

HERE LIES
MYSELF

GRAVESTONE IN ST THOMAS CEMETERY - Ann Arbor, MICH
MYSELF IS THE FAMILY NAME

THE SALUTE of OMAR KHAYYAM

OMAR'S TOMB IS IN NISHAPUR, Persia
And as he predicted:

"MY TOMB SHALL BE IN A SPOT WHERE THE NORTHWIND MAY SCATTER PETALS OF ROSES OVER IT"

A CUTTING FROM THE ROSEBUSH OVER OMAR'S GRAVE WAS TRANSPLANTED TO **FITZGERALD'S GRAVE** AND NOW THE ROSE PETALS ALSO FALL ON THE GRAVE OF HIS TRANSLATOR IN SUFFOLK, England

EVERYTHING HERE
IS EXACT TO MY WISHES
BECAUSE NO ONE EATS
THERE IS NO WASHING OF DISHES

EPITAPH IN A CEMETERY AT PEMBROKE, Mass.

FAREWELL STREET
Newport, R.I.
ENDS AT 4 CEMETERIES

BEER BARREL TOMBSTONE
Kirkheaton, England

THE NON-REVOLVING GRAVES
OF Hokkaido, Japan

ALL AINUS ARE BURIED WITH THEIR FACE TO THE WEST (WHENCE SALVATION IS DUE TO COME) WITH A FORKED BRANCH IN THEIR HAND. IF THE DEAD MAN TURNS IN HIS GRAVE THE STICK TURNS ALSO - AND HIS RELATIVES KNOW WHEN TO STRAIGHTEN HIM OUT!

GRAVESTONES of the Gold Tribe of Siberia
ARE EXACT REPLICAS OF THE
HOMES OF THE DEPARTED!
THEY BELIEVE THE FAMILIAR
SURROUNDINGS WILL KEEP
THEIR SOULS HAPPY

GRAVES SIDE BY SIDE
Chickasaw County Cemetery, MISSISSIPPI

ALL
BALINESE COFFINS
ARE CARVED
IN THE
FORM OF
ANIMALS

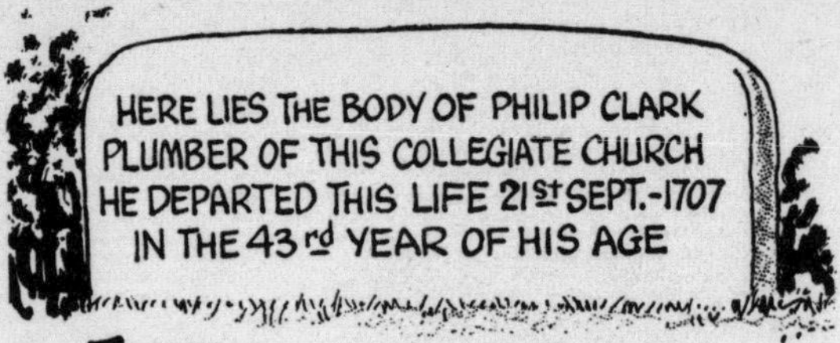
HERE LIES THE BODY OF PHILIP CLARK
PLUMBER OF THIS COLLEGIATE CHURCH
HE DEPARTED THIS LIFE 21st SEPT.-1707
IN THE 43rd YEAR OF HIS AGE

TOMB OF A HUMBLE PLUMBER
in Westminster Abbey

GER
1833

GRAVESTONE
FOUND INSIDE A TREE
Carlisle, Indiana

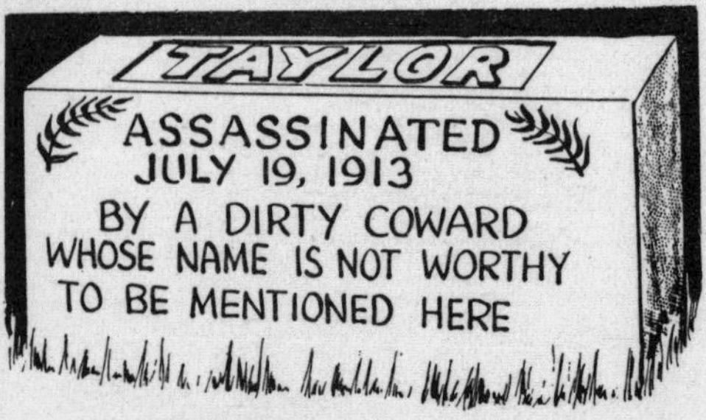
TAYLOR
ASSASSINATED
JULY 19, 1913
BY A DIRTY COWARD
WHOSE NAME IS NOT WORTHY
TO BE MENTIONED HERE

TOMBSTONE
in Oak Hill Cemetery, Tama, Iowa

HE DRANK, HE SANG WHILE HERE ON EARTH
LIVED HAPPY AS A LORD
AND NOW HE HATH RESIGNED HIS BREATH
SO REST NOW PADDY WARD

EPITAPH in the Old Churchyard Mavne, Ireland

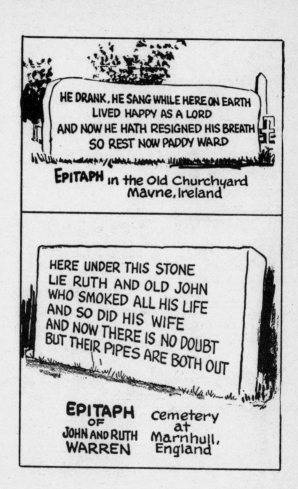

HERE UNDER THIS STONE
LIE RUTH AND OLD JOHN
WHO SMOKED ALL HIS LIFE
AND SO DID HIS WIFE
AND NOW THERE IS NO DOUBT
BUT THEIR PIPES ARE BOTH OUT

EPITAPH OF JOHN AND RUTH WARREN cemetery at Marnhull, England

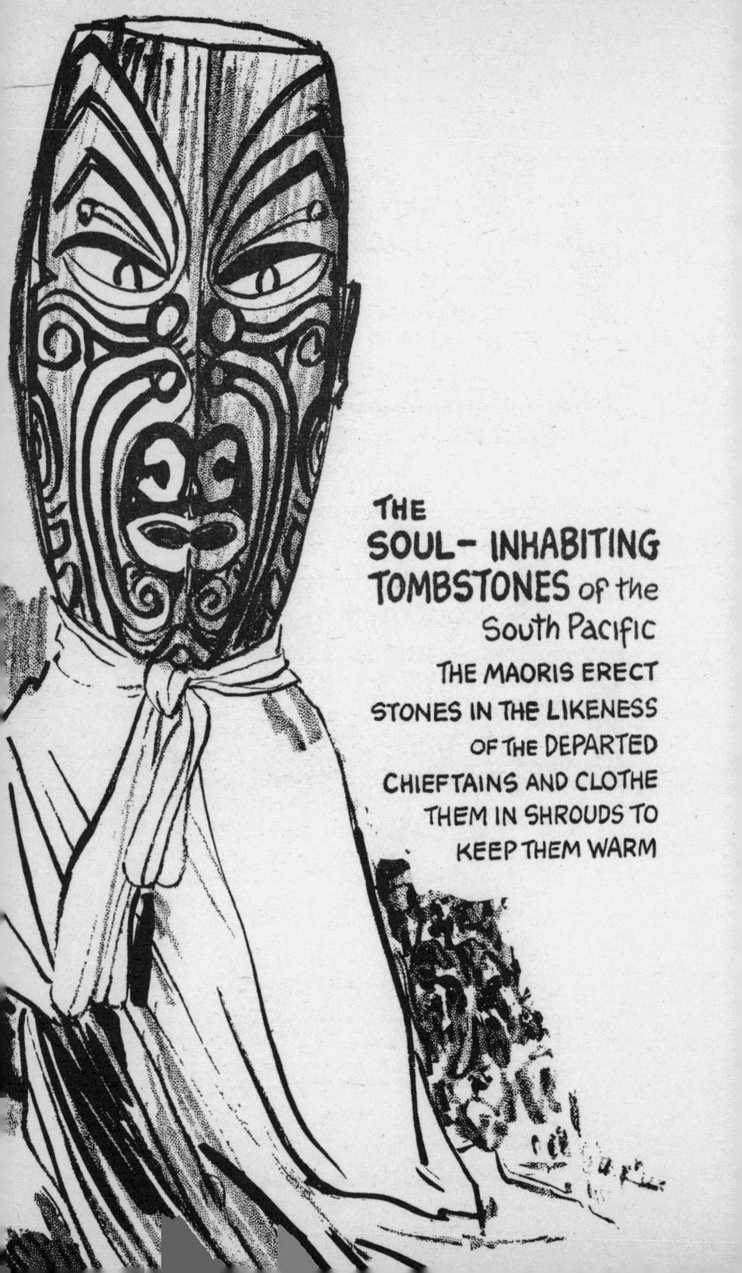
THE
SOUL- INHABITING
TOMBSTONES of the
South Pacific
THE MAORIS ERECT
STONES IN THE LIKENESS
OF THE DEPARTED
CHIEFTAINS AND CLOTHE
THEM IN SHROUDS TO
KEEP THEM WARM

LIVING GRAVES IN NEW GUINEA

WHEN A NATIVE CHIEF DIES HIS BODY IS SEALED IN A LIVING TREE IF THE TREE CONTINUES TO BLOOM IT IS A SIGN HIS SOUL IS RESTING WELL IN HEAVEN

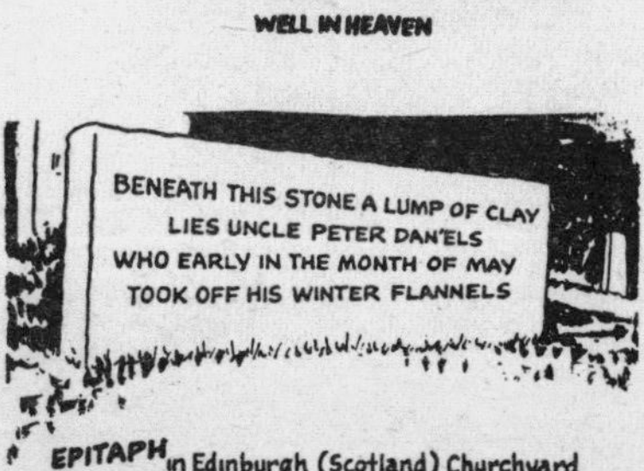
BENEATH THIS STONE A LUMP OF CLAY
LIES UNCLE PETER DAN'ELS
WHO EARLY IN THE MONTH OF MAY
TOOK OFF HIS WINTER FLANNELS

EPITAPH in Edinburgh (Scotland) Churchyard

TOMBSTONES
OF THE ACHAYAK TRIBE
India
ALWAYS
DEPICT THE DECEASED
RIDING TO HEAVEN
ON HORSEBACK!

A RICH MAN IS SHOWN RIDING 2 HORSES

THIS IS THE GRAVE OF
DICK
THE BEST OF BIRDS

TOMBSTONE
ERECTED BY
CHARLES DICKENS
FOR HIS PET CANARY

LEE
LEE

GRAVESTONE OF LEE LEE
LEE COUNTY, MISS.

EACH YUGOSLAVIAN **GRAVE**

USUALLY CONTAINS A DOZEN CROSSES TO DISCOURAGE THE ANGEL OF DEATH FROM TAKING ANY MORE LIVES BY GIVING THE IMPRESSION THAT THE CEMETERY IS FULL!

THE MOST ROMANTIC MEMORIAL IN THE U.S.A.

THE CHURCH OF THE WILDERNESS near Ligonier, Pa., A REPLICA OF THE TOMB OF RACHEL IN THE HOLY LAND. WAS BUILT BY JAMES ROSS MELLON IN 1925 IN LOVING MEMORY OF HIS WIFE
- WHO WAS NAMED RACHEL

LARGE
MARBLE
"TOM AND JERRY" PUNCH BOWL
SERVES AS A GRAVESTONE
LONE FIR CEMETERY, PORTLAND, Oregon

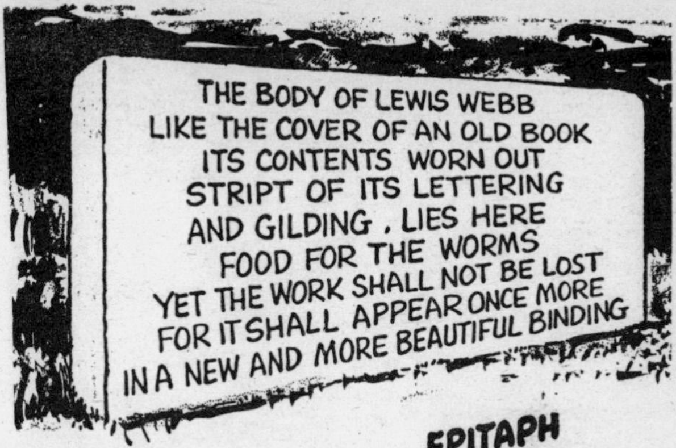
THE BODY OF LEWIS WEBB
LIKE THE COVER OF AN OLD BOOK
ITS CONTENTS WORN OUT
STRIPT OF ITS LETTERING
AND GILDING . LIES HERE
FOOD FOR THE WORMS
YET THE WORK SHALL NOT BE LOST
FOR IT SHALL APPEAR ONCE MORE
IN A NEW AND MORE BEAUTIFUL BINDING

EPITAPH
OF A
BOOKBINDER
Lowestoft
Cemetery.
England

ONCE I WASN'T-
THEN I WAS-
NOW I AIN'T
AGAIN

GRAVESTONE IN
LEE CO. MISS. CEMETERY

MR.
LAW
MRS.
LAWLESS

GRAVESTONES
SIDE BY SIDE—Lee County, Miss.

MONUMENT TO A WOMAN WHO DIED DRINKING 2 GALLONS OF SEA WATER AS A SACRIFICE TO THE SEA GOD OF OKINAWA. SHE IS WORSHIPPED AS A GODDESS

EYES
HERE BLESS MY I I I I
HERE I LIES
IN A SAD PICKLE
KILLED BY AN ICICLE

EPITAPH in Bampton Cemetery
Levonshire, England

ED. W.
WHITESIDE
BORN
APRIL 12, 1864
DIED
APRIL 12, 1930
MRS. E.W.
WHITESIDE
BORN
JUNE 23, 1877
DIED
JUNE 23, 1908

HUSBAND AND WIFE DIED ON THEIR BIRTHDAY

Riverside Cemetery - Asheville, N.C.

In Memory of
ELLEN SHANNON
Aged 26
FATALLY BURNED
1870
BY THE EXPLOSION
OF A LAMP FILLED
WITH DANFORTH'S
NON-EXPLOSIVE FLUID

GRAVESTONE IN GIRARD, Pa.

WHAT THEY GAVE
THEY HAVE
WHAT THEY LEFT
THEY LOST

TOMB OF ROBERT AND MARY MORGAN
Mapperton, England

CANTON --- CHINA

THE SPOT WHERE ALL THE CHINESE OF AMERICA STATE IN THEIR WILLS THAT THEIR BONES MUST LIE.

TRADITION DECREES CHINESE MUST RETURN TO THE LAND OF THEIR ANCESTORS AND ONCE EVERY 10 YEARS THE BONES OF THE DEAD ARE SHIPPED BACK TO CHINA

GRAVESTONE OF ARTHUR HAINE
AN ATHEIST
Vancouver, Canada

THANKFUL
LOSS

GRAVESTONE OF THANKFUL RIPLEY LOSS
WOODTICK CEMETERY, Wolcott, Conn.

PAYNE
AND
JOY

TOMBSTONE
in Garretsville, Ohio,

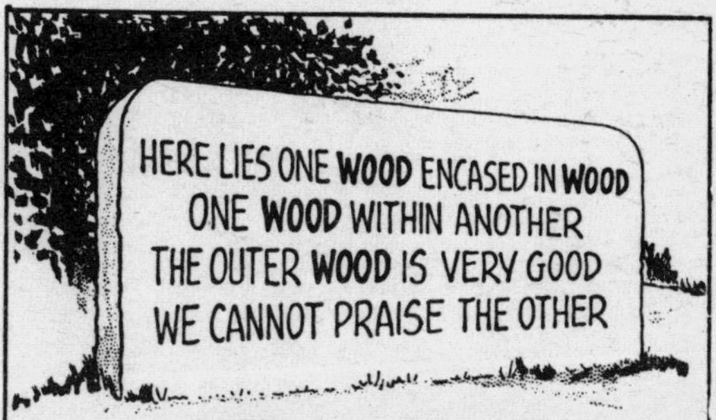
HERE LIES ONE WOOD ENCASED IN WOOD
ONE WOOD WITHIN ANOTHER
THE OUTER WOOD IS VERY GOOD
WE CANNOT PRAISE THE OTHER

EPITAPH IN A CEMETERY
near Winslow, Maine

HORSES
in rural sections of Iceland
ARE ESPECIALLY TRAINED TO SERVE AS "PALLBEARERS."
THEY ARE TAUGHT TO CARRY A COFFIN WITH APPROPRIATE DISPLAY OF MAJESTY AND SORROW

THE TOMB of a HORSE

AN ELABORATE CRYPT BUILT BY AKBAR THE GREAT FOR HIS FAVORITE HORSE—*WHICH THE MOGUL EMPEROR ORDERED BURIED WHERE IT FELL IN BATTLE*

YAGER
REGAY

TOMBSTONE IN WHICH THE NAME IS SPELLED BOTH FORWARD AND BACKWARD
Mt. Hope Cemetery
Hastings-on-Hudson, N.Y.

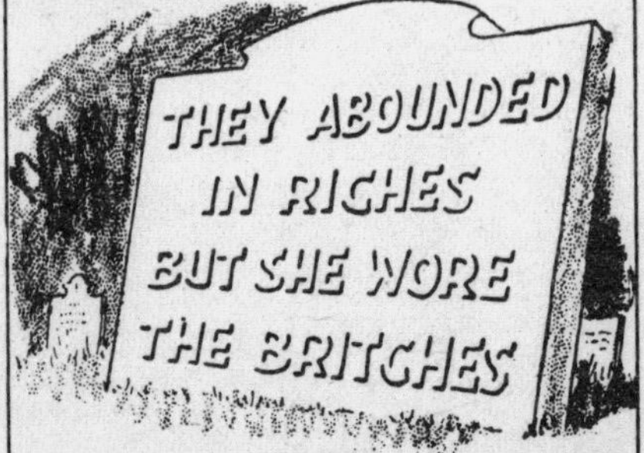
THEY ABOUNDED
IN RICHES
BUT SHE WORE
THE BRITCHES

EPITAPH IN THE CHURCHYARD
at Essex, England

THE MOST ELABORATE TOMBSTONE IN THE WORLD

THE GRAVE MARKER OF THE RAGGIO FAMILY IN THE CEMETERY of Genoa, Italy, IS A 3-STORY HIGH REPLICA OF THE CATHEDRAL OF MILAN

-COMPLETE IN EVERY DETAIL

A BATAK CRYPT
in Sumatra, Indonesia
IS DECORATED WITH THE STUFFED SKIN OF THE GOAT CONSUMED AT THE FUNERAL FEAST—SO THE ANIMAL AND THE DECEASED ***WILL BOTH BE REMEMBERED BY VISITORS TO THE GRAVE***

WAITING
FOR FURTHER
ORDERS

SOLDIER'S GRAVE
IN TIOGA CO., PENNSYLVANIA

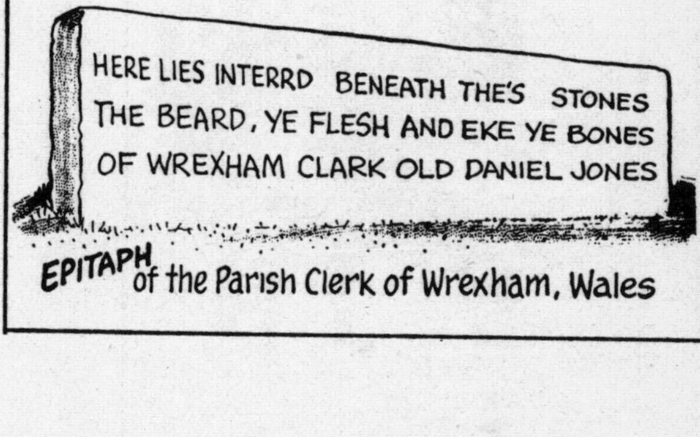
HERE LIES INTERRD BENEATH THE'S STONES
THE BEARD, YE FLESH AND EKE YE BONES
OF WREXHAM CLARK OLD DANIEL JONES

EPITAPH of the Parish Clerk of Wrexham, Wales

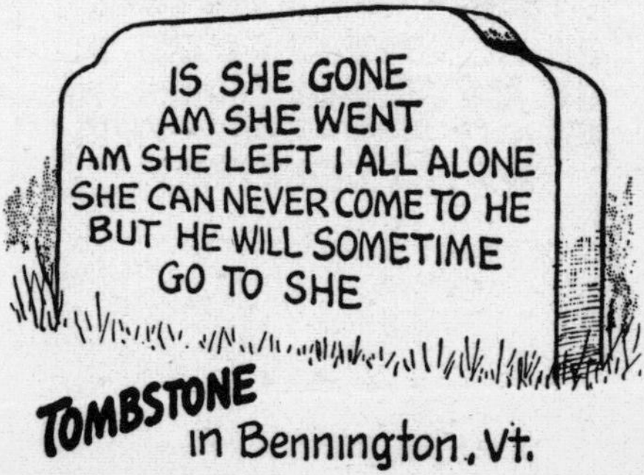
IS SHE GONE
AM SHE WENT
AM SHE LEFT I ALL ALONE
SHE CAN NEVER COME TO HE
BUT HE WILL SOMETIME
GO TO SHE

TOMBSTONE in Bennington, Vt.

THE ISLAND OF THE DEAD

THE ISLAND OF ST. GEORGE IN THE ADRIATIC SEA SERVES THE TOWN OF PERAST, YUGOSLAVIA, ***AS ITS CEMETERY***

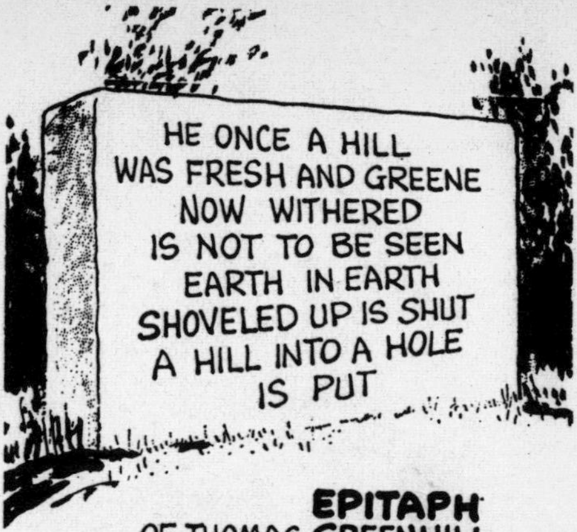
HE ONCE A HILL
WAS FRESH AND GREENE
NOW WITHERED
IS NOT TO BE SEEN
EARTH IN EARTH
SHOVELED UP IS SHUT
A HILL INTO A HOLE
IS PUT

EPITAPH
OF THOMAS **GREENHILL**
in Beddington Church Cemetery
Surrey, England

HERE LIES
EZEKIAL AIKLE
AGE 102
THE GOOD
DIE YOUNG

EAST DALHOUSIE CEMETERY
Nova Scotia

"TO THIS VAIN ORNAMENT - I PREFER DEATH"

INSCRIPTION OF THIS STRANGE STATUE ON THE GRAVE OF FRANCIS II WHO WAS COMPELLED TO RENOUNCE THE IMPERIAL CROWN OF GERMANY 1806

TOMBSTONE OF CECIL CLAY COUNCILOR OF CHESTERFIELD, England

THE INSCRIPTION BENEATH THE 4 C'S READS: "WHAT I WAS I AM"

MEMORIAL TO WORLD WAR I
in Bennwihr, Alsace, France,
WAS THE ONLY THING
UNHARMED BY AN AIR ATTACK
IN WORLD WAR II THAT
DESTROYED THE ENTIRE TOWN

THE STRANGEST TOMBSTONE IN THE WORLD

Otley Churchyard
Yorkshire, England

AN EXACT REPLICA OF THE BRAMHOPE RAILWAY TUNNEL-- BUILT TO MARK THE GRAVES OF WORKMEN KILLED IN AN ACCIDENT IN THAT TUNNEL IN 1849!

THE MAN WHO CARVED HIS OWN TOMBSTONE

BATTY, a surveyor from Bastrop County, Texas, ONE OF 9 MEN SLAIN BY INDIANS IN AN AMBUSH, **WAS THE ONLY ONE WHOSE SKELETON COULD BE IDENTIFIED-** *WITH HIS LAST STRENGTH BATTY HAD CARVED HIS NAME ON THE TREE BENEATH WHICH HE DIED*

HERE LIES
PHILIP SIDNEY
P.S.
THE OLD NUISANCE

GRAVESTONE IN E. CALAIS, Vermont

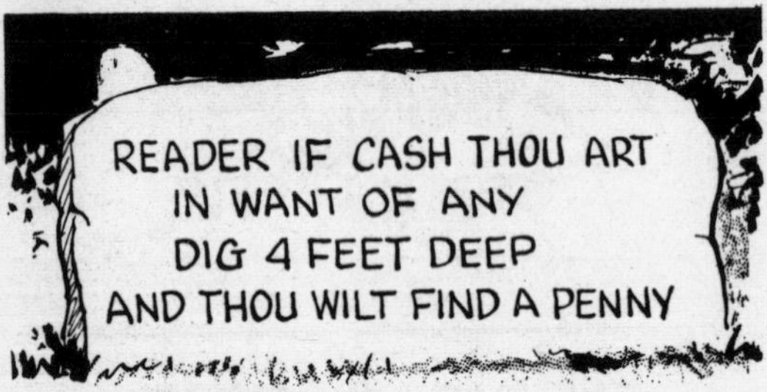
READER IF CASH THOU ART
IN WANT OF ANY
DIG 4 FEET DEEP
AND THOU WILT FIND A PENNY

EPITAPH OF JOHN PENNY.
Wimborne. England

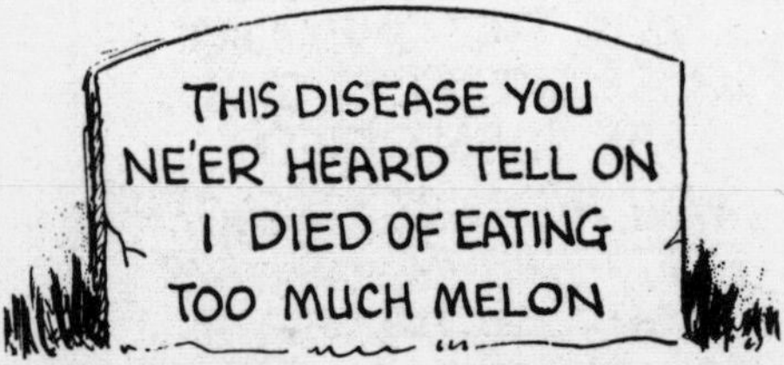
THIS DISEASE YOU
NE'ER HEARD TELL ON
I DIED OF EATING
TOO MUCH MELON

EPITAPH in Chigwell, England

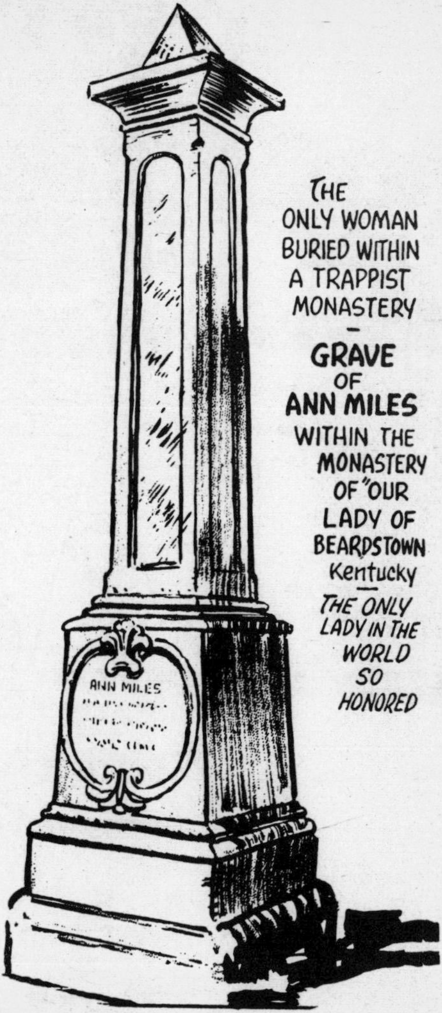

THE
ONLY WOMAN
BURIED WITHIN
A TRAPPIST
MONASTERY
—
GRAVE
OF
ANN MILES
WITHIN THE
MONASTERY
OF "OUR
LADY OF
BEARDSTOWN
Kentucky
—
THE ONLY
LADY IN THE
WORLD
SO
HONORED

THE STRANGEST TAX RETURN IN THE WORLD
GRAVES OF WEALTHY RESIDENTS OF MADAGASCAR ARE DECORATED WITH THE HORNS OF 1/20th OF THEIR HERD OF BULLS--
AS PROOF THAT THEIR KIN MADE THE PROPER DONATION OF MEAT TO THE COMMUNITY'S NEEDY

THE SHORTHAND EPITAPH
tombstone at St. Mary's Church, Sculcoates, England

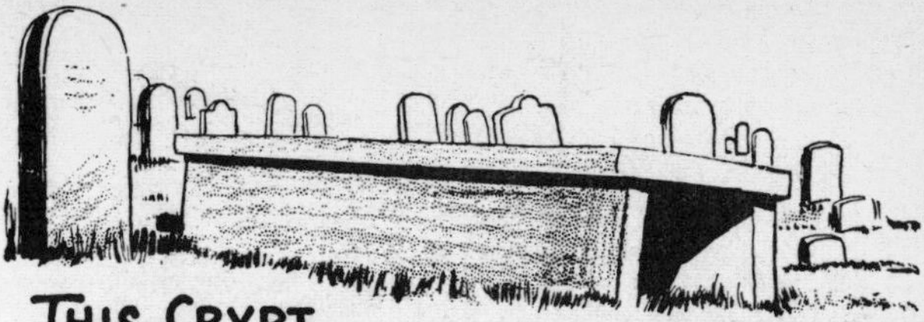

THIS CRYPT in Talbot, Md., WAS LEFT OPEN AT BOTH ENDS ON ORDERS OF THE DECEASED -***WHO INSISTED ON AN ESCAPE ROUTE FROM SATAN***

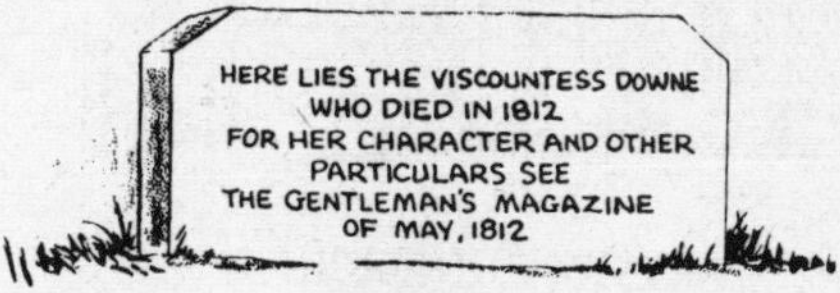
HERE LIES THE VISCOUNTESS DOWNE
WHO DIED IN 1812
FOR HER CHARACTER AND OTHER
PARTICULARS SEE
THE GENTLEMAN'S MAGAZINE
OF MAY, 1812

EPITAPH in The Minster, York, England

SHE
WAS MORE
TO ME
THAN I
EXPECTED

GRAVESTONE IN LEBANON, ILL.

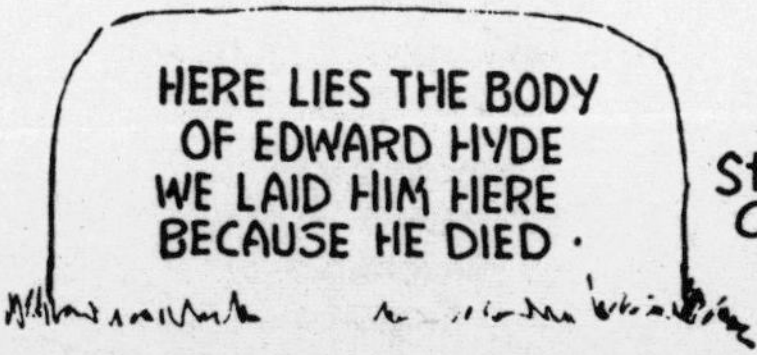
HERE LIES THE BODY
OF EDWARD HYDE
WE LAID HIM HERE
BECAUSE HE DIED.

Epitaph IN Storrington Churchyard, England

THE TOMBSTONE CHURCH

THE CHURCH OF THE HOLY CRUCIFIX
in Milan, Italy
60 FT. BY 40 FT. IN SIZE—*CONSISTS ENTIRELY OF TOMBSTONES FROM AN OLD CEMETERY*
EVEN THE CHURCH BELLS WERE CAST IN BRONZE REMOVED FROM THE TOMBS

THE TOMBSTONE OF JAKOB KORN in Leonberg, Germany, HAS A PANORAMA OF THE TOWN ENGRAVED UPON IT *TO COMMEMORATE THE FACT THAT HE HELD A MORTGAGE ON EVERY BUILDING IN THE COMMUNITY*

THE HIGHEST HUMAN GRAVE
WILSON EVERETTS - Mountain Climber
IS BURIED ON THE TOP
OF MT. ORIZABA, Mexico
18,564 Feet High

HERE LIES THE BODY
OF MARGARET BENT
SHE KICKED UP HER HEELS
AND AWAY SHE WENT

EPITAPH in Winterborn Steepleton
Cemetery
Dorsetshire, England

THE TIPSY TOMBSTONES
Chile
THE GRAVE OF AN ARAUCANIAN IS MARKED BY A POLE CARVED IN HIS LIKENESS-- OVER WHICH HIS KIN DAILY POUR HUGE DRAUGHTS OF CHICHA BEER!
THEY FEEL THEY HAVE APPEASED THE DEPARTED SPIRIT'S THIRST ONLY WHEN THE BEER HAS SO LOOSENED THE SOIL THAT THE MONUMENT BEGINS TO LEAN

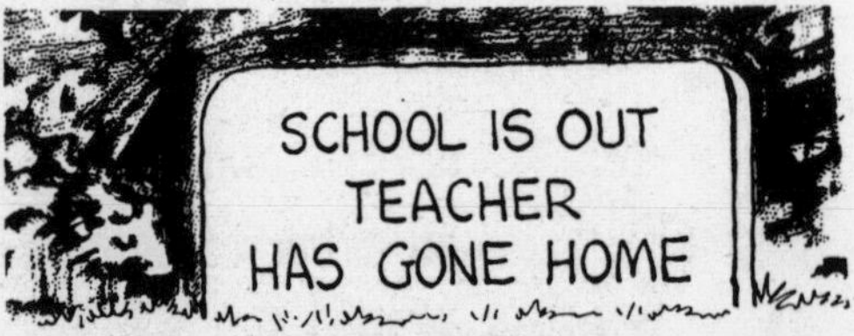
SCHOOL IS OUT
TEACHER
HAS GONE HOME

GRAVE OF PROF. S. B. McCRACKEN
Elkhart, Ind.

TOMBSTONES SIDE BY SIDE!
Coupar Angus, Perthshire, Scotland

THE TOMB OF THE CAMEL
Tibba, India
IT WAS ERECTED OVER THE GRAVE OF A CAMEL NAMED "MELU" WHICH DAILY CARRIED A BEGGING BOWL FROM DOOR TO DOOR *COLLECTING GRAIN FOR CHARITY*

The ATOMIC GRAVESTONES OF NAGASAKI, Japan

THE BOMB DESTROYED THE BUILDINGS AND EVERYTHING AROUND – *BUT LEFT THESE TWO WALLS STANDING LIKE GRAVESTONES*

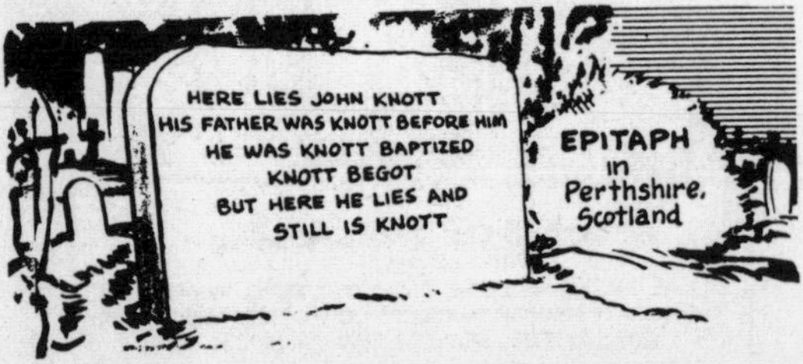
HERE LIES JOHN KNOTT
HIS FATHER WAS KNOTT BEFORE HIM
HE WAS KNOTT BAPTIZED
KNOTT BEGOT
BUT HERE HE LIES AND
STILL IS KNOTT
EPITAPH in Perthshire, Scotland

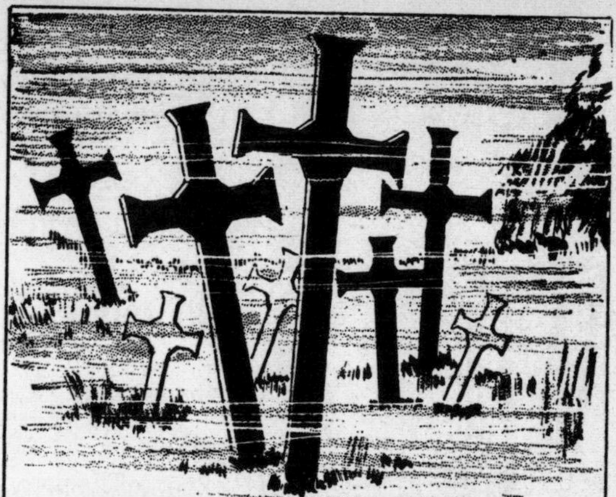

THE SUBMARINE CEMETERY
THE "CEMETERY OF THE DROWNED ONES"
in Concarneau, France
IS COMPLETELY SUBMERGED
EACH TIME THE TIDE RISES
IN FOREST BAY

TOMBSTONE OF 3 BROTHERS
BURIED IN ONE GRAVE
Lockwood, Yorks., England

THE TWO-HEADED TOMBSTONES OF THE KONYAK NAGAS
India

GRAVE MARKERS ARE CARVED IN THE LIKENESS OF THE DEPARTED AND TOPPED BY THE MAN'S OWN SKULL ***SO TRIBESMEN CAN BE DOUBLY CERTAIN THEY ARE MOURNING AT THE RIGHT GRAVE***

HERE LIES
LESTER MOORE
FOUR SLUGS
FROM A FORTY-FOUR
NO LES
NO MOORE

EPITAPH in Boot Hill Cemetery
Tombstone, Ariz.

LULU
PARKER

A BUNCH OF SCALLIONS
WAS CARVED BY FRANK PARKER
ON HIS WIFE'S TOMBSTONE
Rienzi Cemetery
Fond du Lac, Wisc.

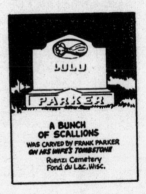

HERE LIES
A
DEAR RELIC
OF THE
GREAT CHICAGO FIRE

Rose Hill Cemetery
Chicago, Ill.

THE COFFIN MEN of BORNEO
THE BRIAN TRIBE ALWAYS CARRY
A JAR WHICH SERVES AS A COFFIN
SHOULD DEATH OVERTAKE THEM
THEY HAVE A HORROR OF BEING BURIED
IN THE BARE GROUND

HERE IS WHERE HE
STOPPED LAST
J. S. JACOBS

SUITCASE GRAVESTONE
OVER A TRAVELING
SALESMAN'S GRAVE
Lincoln, Neb.

ANVIL FASHIONED IN STONE STANDS OVER THE GRAVE OF A BLACKSMITH IN HEADCORN, ENGLAND. All Tools of His Craft have been Minutely Commemorated.

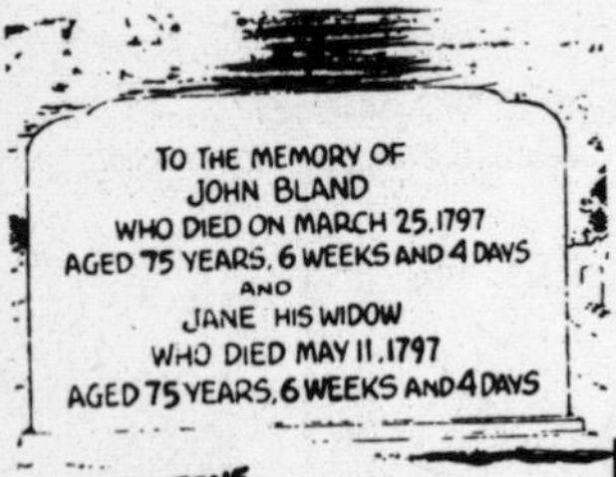
TO THE MEMORY OF
JOHN BLAND
WHO DIED ON MARCH 25, 1797
AGED 75 YEARS, 6 WEEKS AND 4 DAYS
AND
JANE HIS WIDOW
WHO DIED MAY 11, 1797
AGED 75 YEARS, 6 WEEKS AND 4 DAYS

TOMBSTONE in Falkingham, England

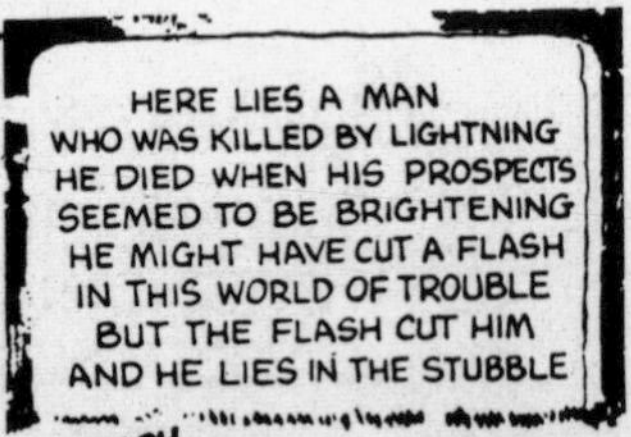
HERE LIES A MAN
WHO WAS KILLED BY LIGHTNING
HE DIED WHEN HIS PROSPECTS
SEEMED TO BE BRIGHTENING
HE MIGHT HAVE CUT A FLASH
IN THIS WORLD OF TROUBLE
BUT THE FLASH CUT HIM
AND HE LIES IN THE STUBBLE

EPITAPH in Great Torrington, England

PRESIDENT'S GRAVEYARD!

PLOT OF GROUND WITH A HIGH WALL
BUILT OF PERFECTLY QUARRIED STONE OF IMMENSE SIZE
WAS DEEDED TO THE PRESIDENTS OF THE UNITED STATES
AS LONG AS THE NATION EXISTS
BY NATHANIEL WILSON JR. IN 1817 Lancaster, Ohio

THE TOMBSTONE PERGOLA
Galt, Ontario
AN ARBOR 48 FEET LONG
MADE FROM 146 TOMBSTONES

THE PORTABLE TOMBS OF PADANG

Indonesia

CRYPTS HOLDING THE BODIES OF UNMARRIED CHILDREN ARE ALWAYS TAKEN ON FAMILY JOURNEYS *TO KEEP THEIR SOULS FROM FEELING NEGLECTED!*

Cemetery plot in New London, Conn.

THE TOMB OF ZEUS ON MT. IUKTAS, Crete.

THE ISLAND OF CRETE IS BOTH THE BIRTHPLACE
AND FINAL RESTING PLACE OF ZEUS.
IT IS BELIEVED THAT WHEN THE FATHER OF THE GODS CHOSE THIS MOUNTAIN FOR HIS LAST RESTING PLACE IT CHANGED ITS SHAPE TO RESEMBLE THE FACE OF ZEUS.

GRAVESTONES — Nassau, N.Y.

THE AURACANIANS
of Chile
CARVE STEPS IN THEIR TOMBSTONES
TO AID THEIR SOULS IN THE ASCENT TO HEAVEN!

THE GRAVE OF THE GIANT
Penrith Churchyard, England

—

THE TOMB OF SIR HUGH CAESARIUS
an English knight
FROM HEAD TO FOOT STONE
MEASURES 14 FEET!

THE TOMB OF CYRUS THE GREAT
FOUNDER OF THE PERSIAN EMPIRE
located in Pasargadae, Iran,
HAS BEEN THE RESIDENCE OF A
SUCCESSION OF FORTUNE TELLERS
FOR 2,000 YEARS

SAFE DEPOSIT BOX of the CELEBES
THE TOMBS of the TIMBUKAR ARE USED TO STORE THE FAMILY JEWELS AND HEIRLOOMS

NO NATIVE WOULD DARE DESPOIL ONE OF THESE GIGANTIC COFFINS

THE PERPETUAL HOST
LIAI-HO of Kota Raja, Sumatra,
DIED IN 1926 – BUT A COMPLETE DINNER FOR 3 PERSONS IS SERVED ON HIS GRAVE AT NOON EACH DAY!

THE MAN WHO WAS NEVER SICK!

THE TOMBSTONE OF SIR THOMAS PARKYNS (1664-1741) FEATURES A STATUE OF HIM IN WRESTLING POSE **AT THE AGE OF 77!**

HE WAS AN ACTIVE WRESTLER ALL HIS LIFE AND NEVER SUFFERED THE SLIGHTEST AILMENT

Bunny, England

Here Lies
an Atheist
ALL DRESSED
UP AND NO
PLACE TO GO

GRAVESTONE IN THURMONT, Md.

RA RA RA
ES ET IN
RAM RAM RAM
I I

LATIN REBUS EPITAPH
IT MEANS:
TERRA ES ET IN TERRAM IBIS
(YOU ARE EARTH AND TO EARTH YOU RETURN)
Tombstone in Stuttgart, Germany

EPITAPH OF DR. FELL
Bishop of Oxford Died 1686

I DO NOT LOVE THEE DR. FELL
THE REASON WHY I CANNOT TELL
BUT THIS I'M SURE I KNOW FULL WELL
I DO NOT LOVE THEE DR. FELL

NEBRASKA APTS

APARTMENT HOUSE TRIMMED WITH GRAVESTONES
Nebraska Apts. BROWNSVILLE, Texas

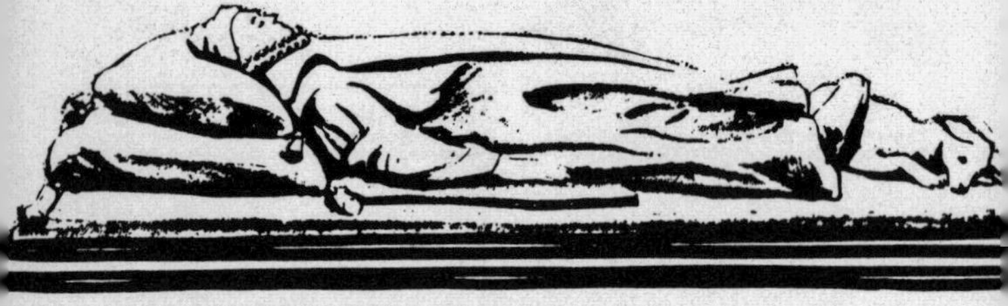

THE PET DOG of WILLIAM THE SILENT,
Ruler of the Netherlands,
REFUSED TO EAT OR DRINK AFTER THE ASSASSINATION OF ITS MASTER-
AND FOLLOWED HIM IN DEATH
(1584)

RAB M^c BETH
WHO DIED FOR THE WANT
OF ANOTHER BREATH
1791-1823

TOMBSTONE
OF A SMUGGLER WHO WAS HANGED
Larne, Ireland

Beneath this Stone Our Baby Lies
He neither Crys or Hollers
He Lived just One and 20 Days
And Cost Us Forty Dollars.

BURLINGTON CEMETERY
Vermont

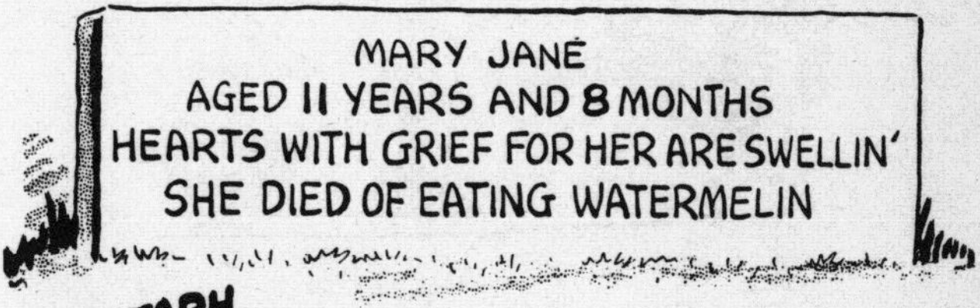
MARY JANE
AGED 11 YEARS AND 8 MONTHS
HEARTS WITH GRIEF FOR HER ARE SWELLIN'
SHE DIED OF EATING WATERMELIN

EPITAPH in Cape May, N.J., cemetery

LORD,
SHE WAS THIN

EPITAPH IN CEMETERY AT TASMANIA, AUSTRALIA

THE STONEMASON FORGOT THE "E" IN THINE

A. DEARMAN
WAS
MY HUSBAND

GRAVESTONE OF THE DEARMAN FAMILY
IN PONTOTOC COUNTY, MISS.

PIANO GRAVESTONE
in the Highgate Cemetery, Eng

WE FANCY NOW HE'D
WISH TO LIVE AGAIN
COULD HE BUT KNOW
WHAT HIS FUNERAL COST

TOMBSTONE
IN ST. GILES' CHURCHYARD
Norwich, Eng.

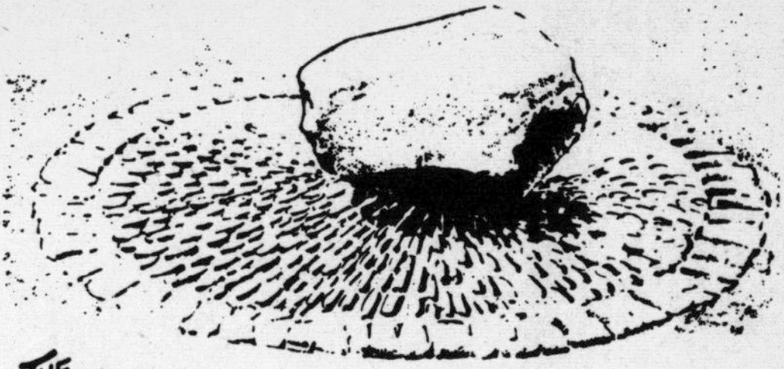

THE BOULDER ON WHICH LLOYD GEORGE USED TO REST IN LIFE IS NOW THE TOMBSTONE BENEATH WHICH HE RESTS IN DEATH (Wales)

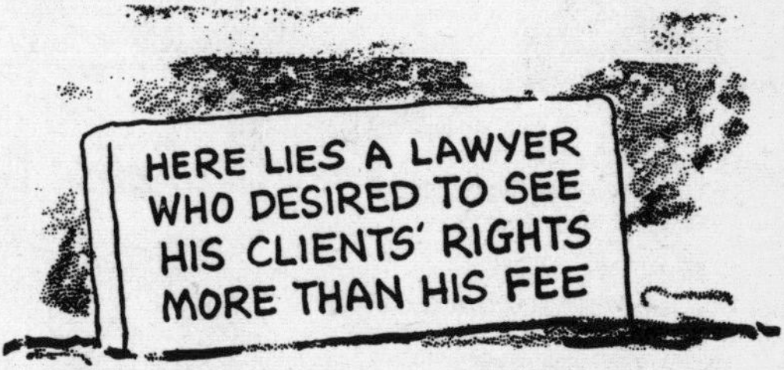
HERE LIES A LAWYER
WHO DESIRED TO SEE
HIS CLIENTS' RIGHTS
MORE THAN HIS FEE

EPITAPH OF ALEXANDER ROLLE
Tavistock Cemetery, England

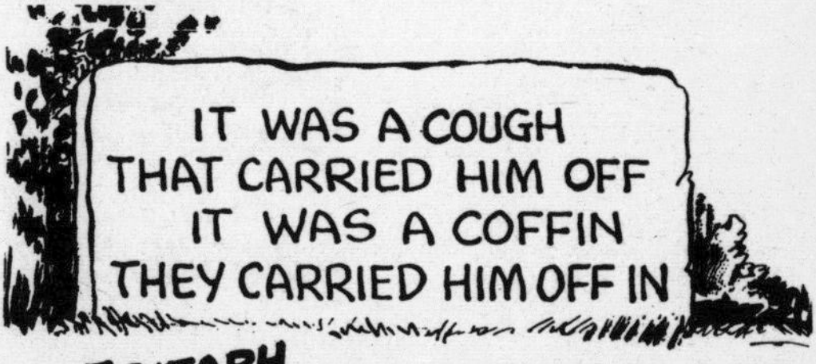
IT WAS A COUGH
THAT CARRIED HIM OFF
IT WAS A COFFIN
THEY CARRIED HIM OFF IN

EPITAPH in the cemetery at Greenwich, Mass.

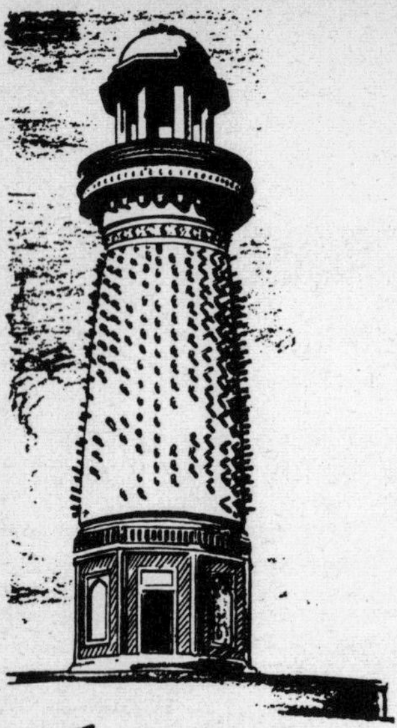

THE STRANGEST SHOOTING BLIND IN THE WORLD!
Fatehpur Sikri, India

A MEMORIAL TOWER
75 FEET HIGH AND STUDDED WITH IVORY TUSKS
BUILT BY EMPEROR AKBAR THE GREAT
OVER THE GRAVE OF
HIS HUNTING ELEPHANT!
AKBAR SHOT DEER FROM ITS TOWER

SON ESPRIT EST
PARTOUT
ET SON COEUR
EST ICI

"HIS SPIRIT IS EVERYWHERE BUT HIS HEART IS HERE"

EPITAPH OVER VOLTAIRE'S HEART
Ferney,
Switzerland

THE DEATH BED TOMBSTONE!

Great Amwell, Hertfordshire, England

WHEN MRS. MARIA PARK MARSHAL DIED –
THE CANOPY OF HER DEATH BED WAS PLACED OVER HER GRAVE!

THE GREAT CANOPY OVER
St. PETER'S TOMB - in Rome
IS SUPPORTED BY
4 BRONZE PILLARS
EACH OF WHICH WEIGHS
EXACTLY 27,948 POUNDS
BUILDER GIANLORENZO BERNINI
PLEDGED HIS PERSONAL
WEALTH AS A GUARANTEE
*THAT THE COLUMNS
WOULD NOT VARY
IN WEIGHT BY
EVEN AN OUNCE*

THE TREE THAT IS ALMOST HUMAN
Nandgat, Bombay

A BANYAN TREE GROWING FROM THE GRAVE
OF A HINDU NAMED RAYAPA
BEARS HIS NAME AND INHERITED HIS WEALTH
RAYAPA HAD PREDICTED THAT SUCH A TREE
WOULD SPRING FROM HIS BODY

THE TOMB OF 18 ECHOES
Bijapur, India

ITS GALLERY REPEATS THE SOUND OF EVERY WHISPER
EXACTLY **18** TIMES -- BECAUSE KING **MUHAMMAD** WAS
DETERMINED EVEN IN DEATH TO HEAR THE VOICES
OF HIS **18 SONS**

MVSCA
SIT TIBI VRNA
LEVIS ET MOLLITER
OSSA QVIESCANT

VIRGIL AT THE FUNERAL OF THE FLY.

THE Roman poet Virgil, (Publius Vergilius Maro) whose bimillennium was celebrated in 1930, spent $100,000 on the burial of his pet fly.

The funeral took place from Virgil's town house on the Esquiline Hill in Rome. The fly was interred amid barbarian splendor and pomp costing more than 800,000 sesterces. The chief mourners were Virgil, Varius, Maecenas and other notables of Octavianus' court. Maecenas delivered a lengthy and eulogistic funeral oration.

Ostentation and eccentricity, as well as the rivalry of display, were the chief motives for this bizarre extravagance of the great poet.

However, this bit of extravagance proved a good investment for Virgil. In the days of the Second Triumvirate all the lands of the idle rich were confiscated and divided among the Roman war veterans. Certain exemptions were made as in the case of grounds and buildings in which someone near and dear was buried, and Virgil was able to claim restitution of his confiscated lands on the basis of his pet fly's interment.

A GRAVESTONE
in Dillstein, Germany,
MARKING THE SPOT IN WHICH
IS BURIED THE **AXE**
WITH WHICH A BROTHER KILLED HIS TWIN

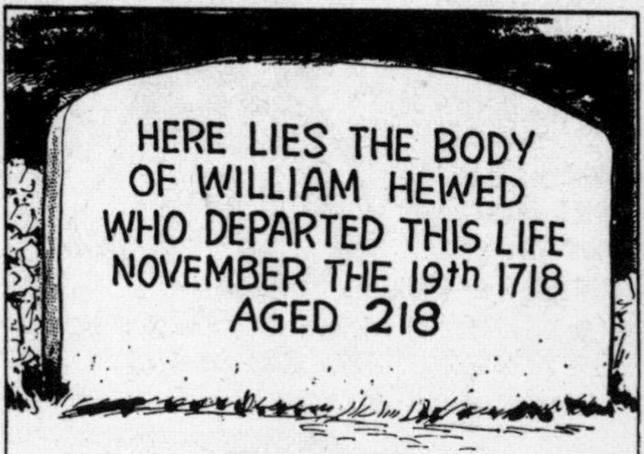
HERE LIES THE BODY
OF WILLIAM HEWED
WHO DEPARTED THIS LIFE
NOVEMBER THE 19th 1718
AGED 218

EPITAPH
in Taddington, England

HOTE
PEPPER
BURNS

GRAVESTONES-SIDE BY SIDE
in MONROE COUNTY, MISSISSIPPI

THE BALUBA ZOO of the DEAD!

WHEN A BALUBA DIES IN THE CONGO HIS SOUL WILL ENTER A WILD ANIMAL (SO THEY BELIEVE) – SINCE WILD ANIMALS ARE DANGEROUS – THEY CONSTRUCT ARTIFICIAL ANIMALS INSTEAD – AND TREAT THEM THE SAME AS LIVING ANIMALS – GIVING THEM FOOD AND DRINK AND WORSHIPPING THEM DEVOTEDLY!

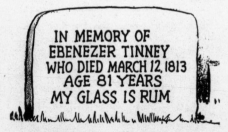

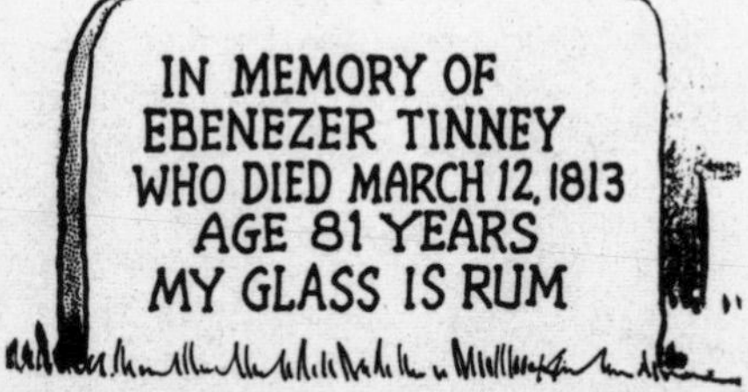
IN MEMORY OF
EBENEZER TINNEY
WHO DIED MARCH 12, 1813
AGE 81 YEARS
MY GLASS IS RUM

EPITAPH in Grafton, Vt.

GRAVESTONE IN Clay County, Miss.

GRAVESTONE IN Clay County, Mississippi

THE TOMBSTONE OF SGT. JOSEPH D. MITCHELL - A CIVIL WAR VETERAN - HAS EMBEDDED IN THE GRANITE BENEATH GLASS ***A HARDTACK BISCUIT*** Greensburg, Kans.

GRAVESTONE IN WOODLAWN CEMETERY WEST PHILADELPHIA Pa

WITCHURCH GRAVEYARD Dorsetshire, Eng.

GRAVESTONE West Point, Miss.

GRAVESTONE IN Tupelo, Miss.

THE CORPSE THAT RODE HORSEBACK FOR 500 MILES!

THE MARQUIS OF PONTLEZ of Quemeneven, France, BANISHED FROM HIS COUNTRY AND FORCED TO FIGHT INFIDELS IN THE HOLY LAND FOR 17 YEARS TO ATONE FOR A SLAYING, CAME HOME TO DIE-AT MARSEILLE HIS COMPANIONS PROPPED HIM IN HIS SADDLE IN FULL ARMOR, AND ALTHOUGH HE DIED THE NEXT DAY, HIS HORSE CARRIED HIM ACROSS FRANCE TO HIS OWN TOWN *THE CORPSE FELL FROM THE SADDLE IN FRONT OF HIS OWN CASTLE -AND THE MARQUIS WAS BURIED THERE WHERE HIS HORSE HALTED*

1355

TOMBSTONES SIDE BY SIDE
Longview Cemetery, Colma, California

DON JUAN'S PENANCE

THE CHURCH OF LA CARIDAD
Seville, Spain
BUILT BY DON MIGUEL MAÑARA – *THE ORIGINAL DON JUAN* – CARRIES THIS EPITAPH: *"HERE LIE THE BONES AND ASHES OF THE WORST MAN WHO EVER LIVED IN THIS WORLD"*

HAPPY HAI KO — THE MERRY MUMMY

of Yunnanfu, China

BY THE AID OF FALSE TEETH HIS MUMMY HAS BEEN GRINNING CONSTANTLY FOR 228 YEARS

WHEN HAI KO THE ABBOT OF YUANG TON PAQ TEMPLE DIED—
HE SPECIFIED THAT HIS BODY BE PRESERVED
WITH A GRIN ON HIS FACE
AS HE WAS CHEERFUL IN LIFE

Warm Summer Sun
Shine Kindly Here
Warm Southern Wind
Blow Softly Here
Green Sod Above
Lie Light, Lie Light
Good Night My Heart
Good Night, Good Night

MARK TWAIN'S EPITAPH FOR HIS DAUGHTER'S TOMBSTONE

Elmira, N.Y.

LET
SLEEPING
DOGS
LIE

EPITAPH IN A DOGS' CEMETERY

Edinburgh, Scotland

HE HAS
ANSWERED
HIS LAST
ALARM

EPITAPH OVER THE GRAVE OF CAPT. WILLIAM P. MONROE OF THE Wilmington, N.C., FIRE DEPARTMENT *WHO WAS KILLED WHILE RACING TO A FIRE*

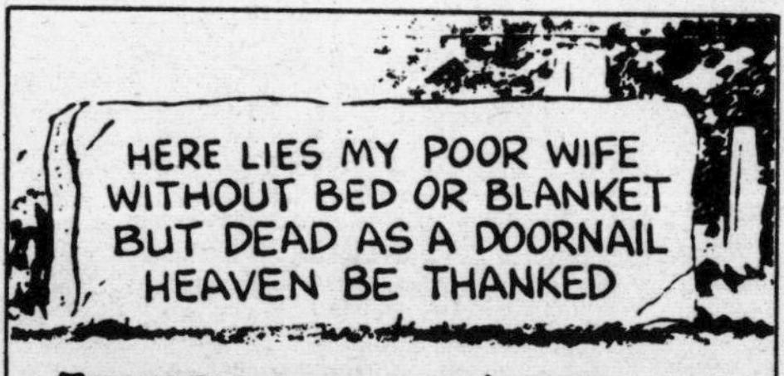
HERE LIES MY POOR WIFE
WITHOUT BED OR BLANKET
BUT DEAD AS A DOORNAIL
HEAVEN BE THANKED

EPITAPH in Storrington, England

A MEMORIAL
ERECTED IN THE Southern Vosges Mountains of France
TO HEROIC MEMBERS OF MINE DISPOSAL SQUADS OF WORLD WAR II
DEPICTS THE PREMATURE EXPLOSION OF A ROAD MINE
WITH A SOLDIER BEING HURTLED TO HIS DEATH

ENDALL CEMETERY

NEAR SYRACUSE, Kansas

THERE IS BURIED HERE
A WILD ELEPHANT
WHO IN DEFENSE OF HIS HERD
CHARGED AND DERAILED A TRAIN
SEPT. 17, 1894

MONUMENT
near Teluk Anson, Malaya

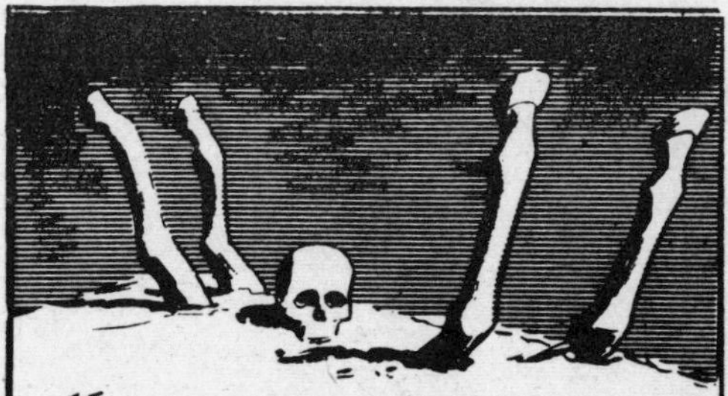

THE STRANGE MONUMENT of the SAHARA
A HORSE AND RIDER
PERISHED IN A SANDSTORM IN
the Tenere Desert, the French Sahara,
AND STILL VISIBLE YEARS LATER
***ARE THE 4 LEGS OF THE HORSE
AND THE SKULL OF ITS RIDER***

The TOMB of the 13th DALAI LAMA of Tibet
ON THE ROOF OF THE POTALA PALACE IN LHASA IS 70 FEET HIGH AND COVERED WITH A SHEET OF SOLID GOLD THAT WEIGHS A TON
AND IS VALUED AT MORE THAN
$1,000,000

LUTZ

TOMBSTONE
OF
WILLIAM LUTZ
--WHO WAS
BORN
LIVED
AND WAS
BURIED
ALL ON THE SAME SPOT!
Rockville, Conn.

KING TAMAFAINGA of Samoa PREPARED HIS OWN GRAVE BY ADDING ONE STONE EACH TIME HE TOOK ANOTHER WIFE! HE DIED AFTER PLACING 99 STONES

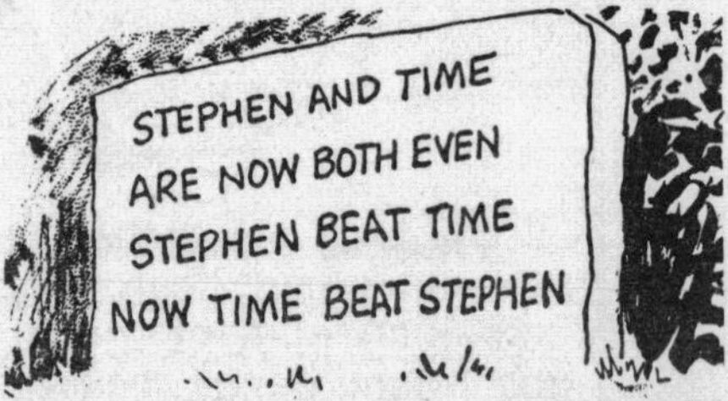
STEPHEN AND TIME
ARE NOW BOTH EVEN
STEPHEN BEAT TIME
NOW TIME BEAT STEPHEN

A FIDDLER'S EPITAPH
in Hadleigh, England

THE CHURCH THAT WAS SPARED
BECAUSE A MONARCH WAS STINGY

THE CATHEDRAL OF PETERBOROUGH
England
ORDERED DESTROYED BY KING HENRY VIII
WAS SPARED AT THE LAST MOMENT
WHEN THE RULER WAS REMINDED THAT
HE WOULD HAVE TO BUILD A SUBSTITUTE CRYPT FOR HIS WIFE

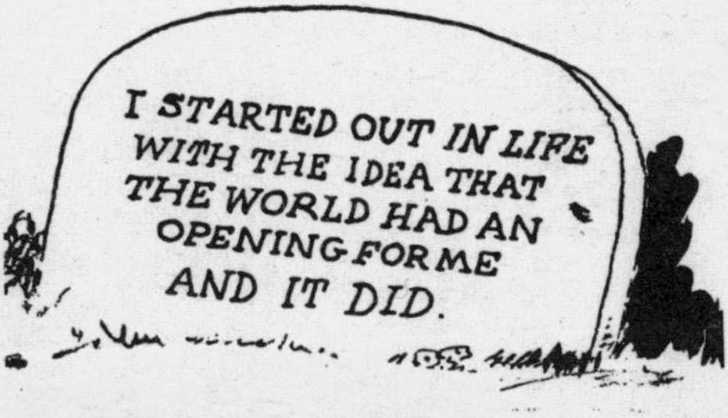
I STARTED OUT IN LIFE
WITH THE IDEA THAT
THE WORLD HAD AN
OPENING FOR ME
AND IT DID.

GRAVESTONE
In Sheffield, England

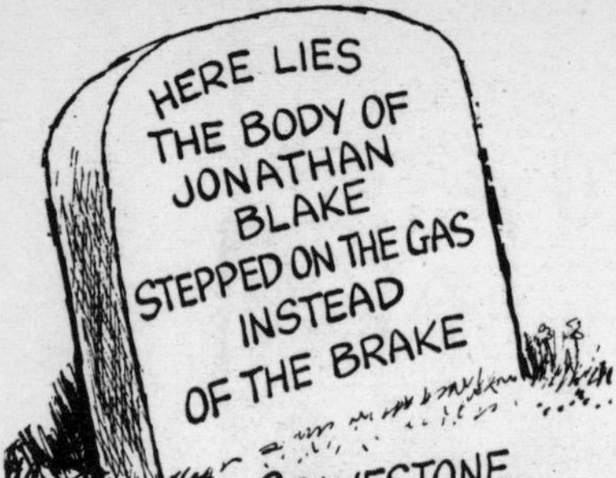
HERE LIES
THE BODY OF
JONATHAN
BLAKE
STEPPED ON THE GAS
INSTEAD
OF THE BRAKE

GRAVESTONE NEAR UNIONTOWN, PA.

MY FORGE AND HAMMER
LIE RECLINED
MY BELLOWS TOO HAVE
LOST THEIR WIND
MY FIRE'S EXTINCT,
MY FORGE DECAYED,
AND IN THE DUST
MY VISE IS LAID.
MY COAL IS SPENT.
MY IRON GONE,
MY ANVIL'S BROKE,
MY WORK IS DONE.

EPITAPH TO A BLACKSMITH
St. Mary's Churchyard
Stonebridge, England

THE TURF HAS DRANK A
WIDOW'S TEAR;
THREE OF HER HUSBANDS
SLUMBER HERE

Epitaph in cemetery
Staffordshire, Eng.

MRS. EVAN
LLEWELLYN
BORN
CHRISTMAS DAY
MARRIED
CHRISTMAS DAY
TAKEN ILL
CHRISTMAS DAY
DIED
CHRISTMAS DAY

GRAVESTONE
IN A PARISH CHURCHYARD
CARMARTHENSHIRE, Wales

LOUISA ADLER
DIED OF GRIEF
CAUSED BY
A NEIGHBOR
NOW RESTS
IN PEACE
1879 1933

TOMBSTONE IN A CEMETERY
- Palm Springs, Calif.

JOHN
ADAMS
THE LIQUOR HE DRANK
BEING TOO MUCH FOR ONE
HE COULD NOT CARRY OFF
- SO HE'S NOW CARRION

Gravestone in Indianapolis

SAMUEL LITTLER
PLANTED THE TREE FROM WHICH
HE MADE HIS OWN COFFIN
WEST CAMDEN, N.Y.

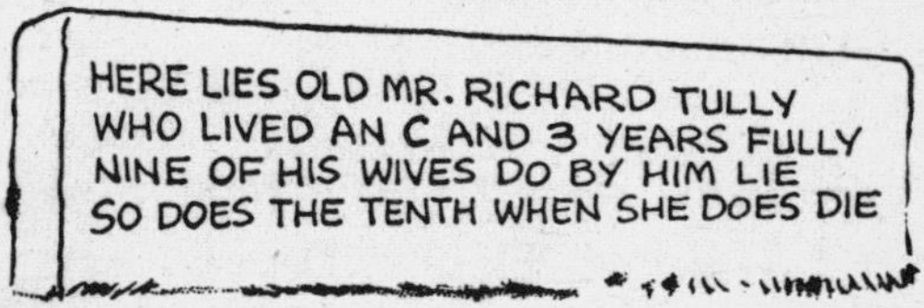
HERE LIES OLD MR. RICHARD TULLY
WHO LIVED AN C AND 3 YEARS FULLY
NINE OF HIS WIVES DO BY HIM LIE
SO DOES THE TENTH WHEN SHE DOES DIE

EPITAPH in St. Katherine's Cemetery - Gloucester, England

THE STRANGE GRAVESTONES OF GRANGEVILLE
California
A CRADLE - A LIFEBOAT AND AN ANCHOR CARVED FROM STONE BY "BLACK HORSE" JONES
TO MARK HIS OWN GRAVE

THREE WIVES OF HENRY MANNING LIE SIDE BY SIDE IN WARRENVILLE, Ill.

MY HEALTHFUL WIFE
MY BELOVED WIFE
MY SWEET WIFE

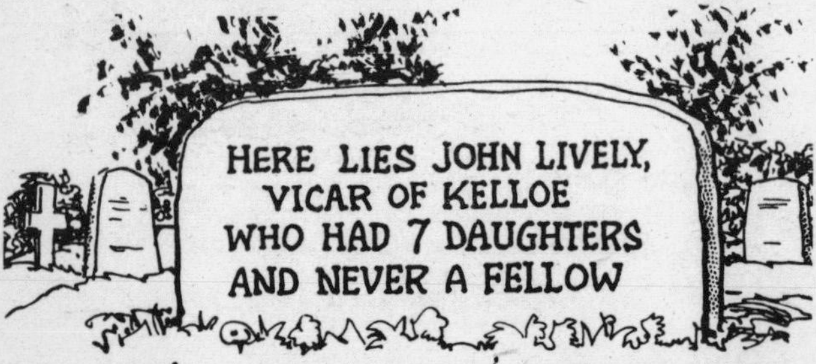
HERE LIES JOHN LIVELY,
VICAR OF KELLOE
WHO HAD 7 DAUGHTERS
AND NEVER A FELLOW

EPITAPH in the cemetery in Kelloe, England

THE MOVING GRAVE! — Srinagar, Kashmir

GRAVE OF A HINDU SAINT MOVES DOWNHILL *ONE* YARD A YEAR

IT HAS MOVED **260** *YARDS SINCE HE WAS BURIED*

IN
MEMORY OF
LIDIA
WIFE OF
SIMEON Palmer
IN
MEMORY OF
ELIZABETH
WHO SHOULD HAVE
BEEN THE WIFE OF
SIMEON Palmer

UNIQUE GRAVESTONES IN LITTLE COMPTON, R.I., CEMETERY

GRAVESTONE OF A CITY

MARKING THE SPOT THAT WAS ONCE *"LA MOTHE"*
A CITY OF 32,000 PEOPLE IN THE VALLEY OF THE MEUSE, France
WHICH WAS TOTALLY DESTROYED BY CARDINAL RICHELIEU IN 1645

ALTHOUGH THE CITY OF LA MOTHE WAS ONLY A TOMBSTONE - IT CONTINUED TO SEND REPRESENTATIVES TO PARLIAMENT IN PARIS FOR 200 YEARS

LIGHTNING SHATTERED THE TOMBSTONE OF T.G.BROWNELL WHO WAS KILLED *BY A BOLT OF LIGHTNING!*

Cemetery at Bovina, Colo.

TEARS
CANNOT RESTORE HER
THEREFORE
DO I WEEP

MACHIAS CEMETERY, Maine

HERE BENEATH THIS
STONE WE LIE
BACK TO BACK MY
WIFE AND I
AND WHEN THE ANGELS
TRUMP SHALL TRILL
IF SHE GETS UP THEN
I'LL LIE STILL!

TOMBSTONE IN BARLININE CEMETERY
Glasgow, Scotland

HERE LIES
JOHN YEAST
PARDON ME
FOR NOT RISING

GRAVESTONE
IN RUIDOSO, N.M.

THE TOMB of ANARKALI
in Lahore, Pakistan,
CONTAINS A WALL IN WHICH A GIRL NAMED ANARKALI WAS *BURIED ALIVE BY INDIAN EMPEROR AKBAR IN 1599 BECAUSE SHE HAD SMILED AT ANOTHER MAN.*
THE "OTHER MAN" WAS THE EMPEROR'S OWN SON, JAHANGIR, WHO BUILT THE MAGNIFICENT TOMB AFTER HIS FATHER'S DEATH

THE CHAPEL OF ST. ORAN
on the island of Iona, in the Hebrides,
HOLDS THE TOMBS OF
48 KINGS of SCOTLAND, 8 KINGS of NORWAY,
4 KINGS of IRELAND and 4 KINGS of FRANCE

The SKYSCRAPER TOMB
—
THE TOMB OF JOHN PETERSEN IS 300 FT. HIGH
—
Southampton, Eng.

PETER CHASE
BORN
AUG. 19, 1832
DIED
JAN. 14, 1894
ANNA CHASE
BORN
AUG 19, 1832
DIED
JAN. 14, 1894

A HUSBAND AND WIFE
BORN THE SAME DAY
AND
DIED THE SAME DAY!
Cemetery in Weems, Va.

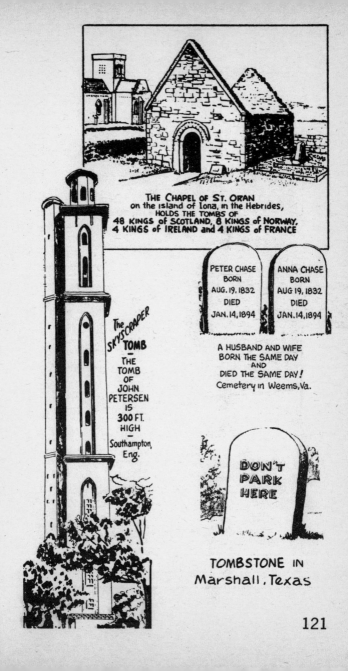

DON'T
PARK
HERE

TOMBSTONE IN
Marshall, Texas

THE **MEMORIAL** in Dartmouth, England, TO THE DEAD OF WORLD WARS I AND II

ORIGINALLY SERVED AS A BAPTISMAL FONT **300 YEARS AGO**

THE **HEADSTONE** ON THE GRAVE OF PLATT R. SPENCER WHOSE STYLE OF WRITING WAS ADOPTED THROUGHOUT AMERICA

BEARS HIS NAME IN HIS OWN SPENCERIAN HAND

Ashtabula County, Ohio

GRAVESTONE

in Mottville Cemetery
Michigan

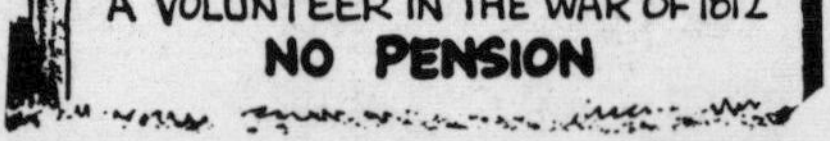
RANSOM BEARDSLEY
DIED JAN. 24, 1850
AGED 56 YEARS, 7 MONTHS, 21 DAYS
A VOLUNTEER IN THE WAR OF 1812
NO PENSION

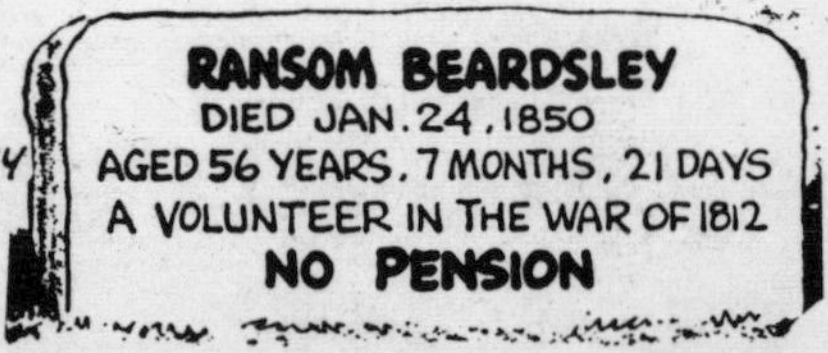

SHE WAS HARD TO BEAT
EPITAPH OF MRS. H. B. CORDES
Cemetery in Cecil County Md.

I WONDER WHERE HE WENT
TOMBSTONE OF DANIEL COLE in Wellsboro, Pa. Cemetery

The GAMBLER'S COFFIN
WILLARD ALDRICH, Mishawaka, Ind.

MADE PROVISION TO BE BURIED SITTING UP BEFORE A CARD TABLE HOLDING A PACK OF CARDS – A BOTTLE OF WHISKEY – PIPE – TOBACCO AND MATCHES. UNDER THE TABLE HE ORDERED PLACED HIS BOOTS, SADDLE AND SHOTGUN.

Died in 1882

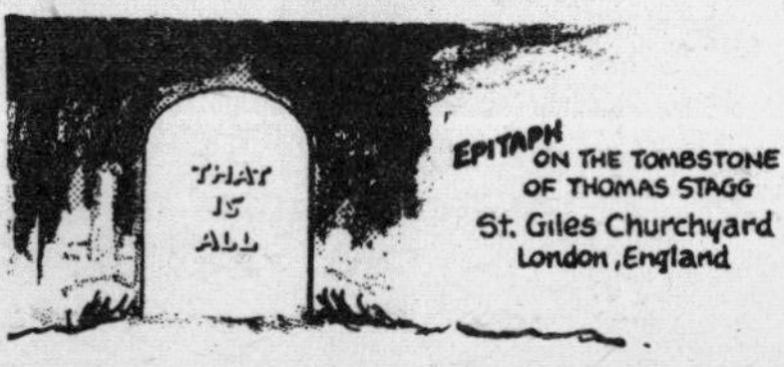
THAT IS ALL
EPITAPH ON THE TOMBSTONE OF THOMAS STAGG
St. Giles Churchyard London, England

THE ELEPHANT HERD THAT AVENGED ITS LEADER!

CHARLES LINDSAY ROSS
A VETERAN BIG-GAME HUNTER OF MPIKA, AFRICA SHOT **250** ELEPHANTS – THE LAST A BIG BULL ELEPHANT THAT KILLED THE HUNTER BEFORE IT DIED

ROSS WAS BURIED IN THE CEMETERY AT MPIKA -- 8 MILES FROM THE SCENE OF HIS DEATH – *AND THAT VERY NIGHT A HERD OF ELEPHANTS INVADED THE CEMETERY AND FLATTENED THE HUNTER'S GRAVE--YET NO OTHER GRAVE BORE EVEN A FOOTPRINT!*

MAY 25, 1938

HERE LIES
A. HUSBAND
THE
HUSBAND
OF
MRS. HUSBAND

ELDORADO, Arkansas

The ORGANIST'S TOMBSTONE!

8 FEET HIGH - COMPLETE IN EVERY DETAIL!

Hampstead Cemetery, London N.W.

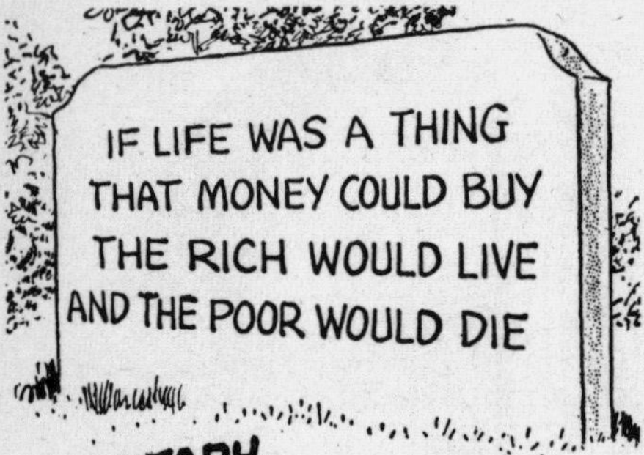
IF LIFE WAS A THING
THAT MONEY COULD BUY
THE RICH WOULD LIVE
AND THE POOR WOULD DIE

EPITAPH in the churchyard of Poling, England

HERE LIES MY 4 HUSBANDS
ALL IN A ROW
AND HERE LET THEM KEEP
WITHOUT MAKING A BOTHER
WHILE I LOOK ABOUT ME
TO FIND ME ANOTHER

TOMBSTONE in Wheldrake Cemetery England

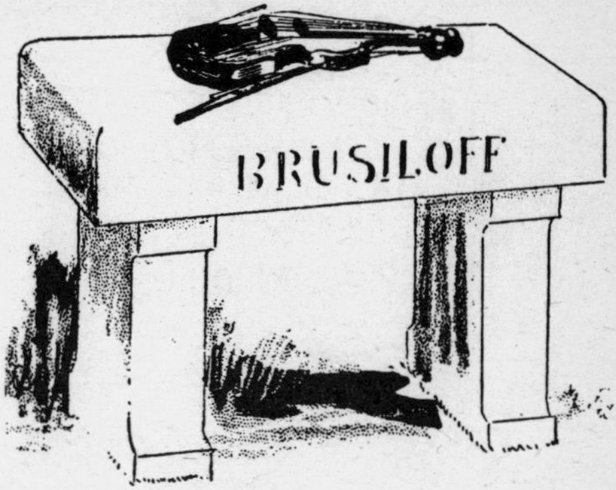

NOVEL GRAVESTONE OF A MUSICIAN

— GRAVESTONE TO A MAN WHO WAS ***BORN AND DIED ON THE SAME DAY OF THE SAME MONTH 100 YEARS LATER***

— Matamoras, Mexico

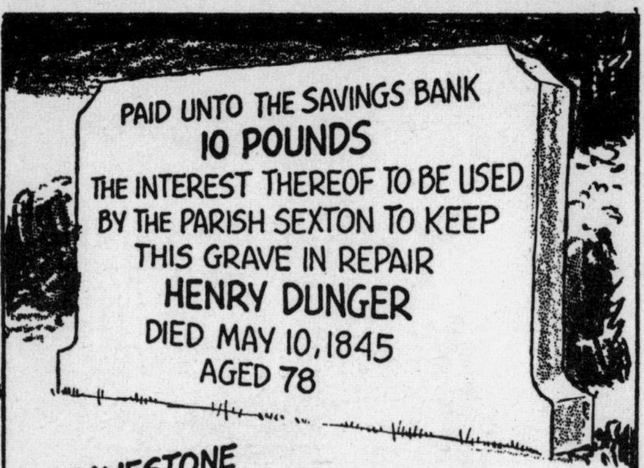
PAID UNTO THE SAVINGS BANK
10 POUNDS
THE INTEREST THEREOF TO BE USED
BY THE PARISH SEXTON TO KEEP
THIS GRAVE IN REPAIR
HENRY DUNGER
DIED MAY 10, 1845
AGED 78

GRAVESTONE in Nunhead Cemetery England

ROTHWELL
WILLIAM P. ROTHWELL M.D.
THIS IS ON ME ℞

GRAVESTONE in Oak Grove Cemetery Pawtucket, R.I.

A 4-POSTER BED WAS SUCH A PROUD POSSESSION OF COUNTESS ALICE of Derby, England, THAT AS HER LAST REQUEST A REPLICA OF IT ADORNS HER TOMB IN THE CHURCH OF HAREFIELD -1636-

THE STRANGEST STUDY HALL IN THE WORLD!
Kara, India

THE TOMB OF MAULANA KHWAJAGI
famed Indian scholar
HAS BEEN VISITED FOR 555 YEARS BY DULL STUDENTS IN THE BELIEF THAT STUDYING 40 DAYS INSIDE ITS WALLS *WILL ASSURE HIGH MARKS IN ANY EXAMINATION*

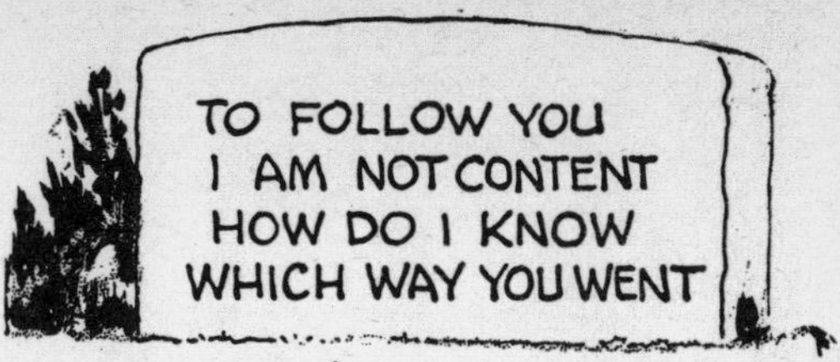
TO FOLLOW YOU
I AM NOT CONTENT
HOW DO I KNOW
WHICH WAY YOU WENT

EPITAPH in the Cemetery at Enfield, Mass.

HONEST JOHN
IS DEAD
AND GONE

EPITAPH in St. John's Churchyard, Worcester, England

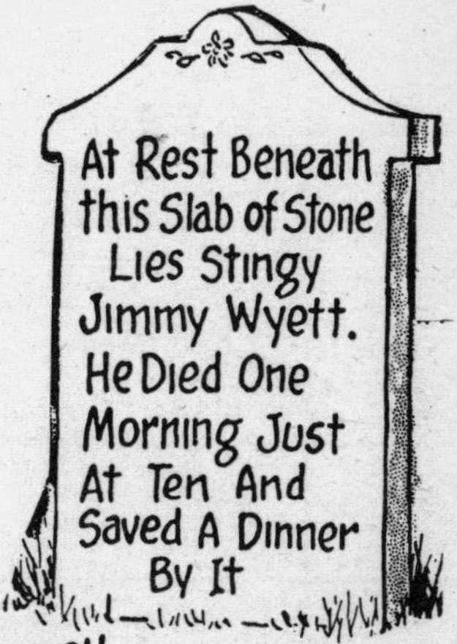
At Rest Beneath
this Slab of Stone
Lies Stingy
Jimmy Wyett.
He Died One
Morning Just
At Ten And
Saved A Dinner
By It

EPITAPH IN A CHURCHYARD Falkirk, England

AT REST
ANNA S. WORK
1824-1896
HERE I LAY
MY BURDEN DOWN,
CHANGE THE CROSS
INTO THE CROWN

TOMBSTONE

Table Rock, Nebraska

COD

GRAVESTONE IN Erie, Colorado

FRAGRANT TOMBSTONE

INCENSE HAS BEEN BURNING 188 YEARS OVER THE GRAVE OF EMPEROR ANG TONG OF ANNAM

THE ANNAMESE NAME FOR CEMETERY IS ***"VALLEY of PERFUME"***

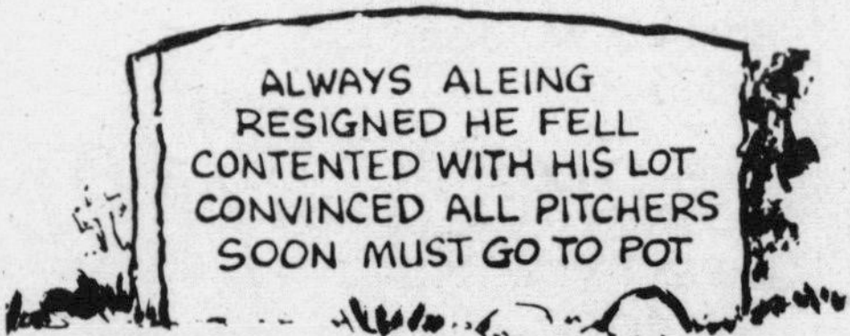

ALWAYS ALEING
RESIGNED HE FELL
CONTENTED WITH HIS LOT
CONVINCED ALL PITCHERS
SOON MUST GO TO POT

EPITAPH OF AN ALEHOUSE KEEPER NAMED PITCHER
Rodmarton, England

NICCOLÓ FONTANA (1506-1559)
WHO BECAME ONE OF THE FOREMOST MATHEMATICIANS OF ALL TIME, WAS SO POOR THAT AT THE AGE OF 6 HE PRACTICED HIS NUMBERS IN A CEMETERY - ***USING TOMBSTONES AS SLATES***

THE Coffin OF ANTHONY BRAGGE of Charmouth, England, AT HIS OWN REQUEST WAS MADE ***FROM HIS DINNER TABLE***

A **GRAVE** in Freiburg, Germany THAT BEARS THE FIGURE OF A SLEEPING GIRL BUT NO NAME, HAS BEEN DECORATED WITH A FRESH BOUQUET OF FLOWERS ***EACH DAY FOR THE LAST 200 YEARS***

PERFECT PEACE
UNTIL
WE MEET AGAIN

GRAVESTONE ERECTED BY A HUSBAND TO HIS WIFE

—Bedford, England

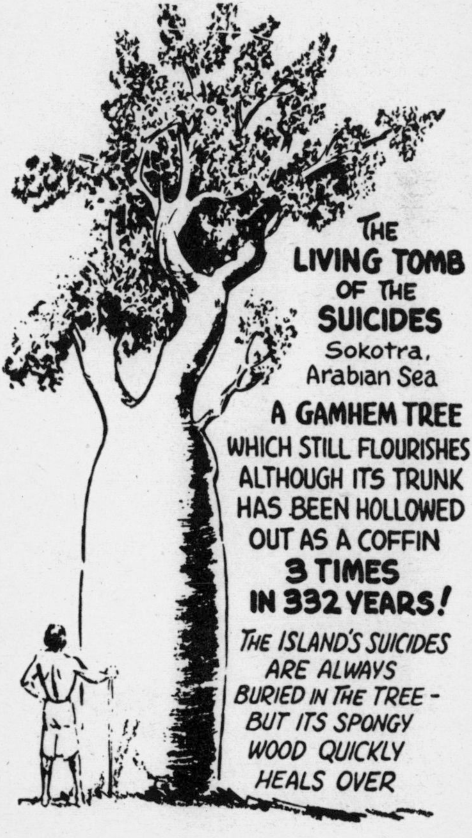
THE LIVING TOMB OF THE SUICIDES
Sokotra, Arabian Sea
A GAMHEM TREE WHICH STILL FLOURISHES ALTHOUGH ITS TRUNK HAS BEEN HOLLOWED OUT AS A COFFIN 3 TIMES IN 332 YEARS!
THE ISLAND'S SUICIDES ARE ALWAYS BURIED IN THE TREE - BUT ITS SPONGY WOOD QUICKLY HEALS OVER

THE LIVING TOMBSTONE

A HOLLOW TREE IN WHICH A POLYNESIAN CHIEF IS BURIED *WITH THE HISTORY OF HIS LIFE AS AN EPITAPH* ***IN TRIBAL HIEROGLYPHICS***

POGINUO SAM ZA
SVOJU DOMOVINU
JA
SAM
OVDE
THE GRAVE OF A NAME!
WHEN A YUGOSLAVIAN SOLDIER DIES FOR HIS COUNTRY
AND HIS BODY CANNOT BE FOUND —
HIS NAME (SPOKEN INTO AN OPEN GRAVE BY A RELATIVE)
IS BURIED INSTEAD! AND A PICTURE OF THE SOLDIER
IS PAINTED ON THE GRAVESTONE WITH THESE WORDS ISSUING
FROM HIS LIPS "I DIED FOR MY COUNTRY I AM HERE"

HIS FOOT IS SLIPT
AND HE DID FALL
HELP, HELP HE CRIED
AND THAT WAS ALL

EPITAPH OF JOSEPH CRAPP
in Mylor Churchyard,
Cornwall, England

Here Lies
SINCE 1904
MARY MORIARTY
ONE OF THE BEST
MOTHERS-IN-LAW
GOD EVER MADE

GRAVESTONE
ST MARY'S CEMETERY
HAMILTON, OHIO

HERE LIES
FLATTENED OUT
THE POSTMAN-
MOLINA

EPITAPH OF A MAILMAN
NAMED MOLINA WHO WAS
CRUSHED BY A LANDSLIDE
Uspallata, Argentina

THE SIDI SAHAB MOSQUE in Kairwan, Tunisia, MARKS THE GRAVE OF A COMPANION OF MOHAMMED *BECAUSE WHEN HE WAS BURIED THERE WERE CONCEALED IN HIS GARMENTS* ***3 HAIRS STOLEN FROM THE PROPHET'S BEARD***

EVERY GRAVE in the Wachersberg Cemetery, Bavaria CARRIES THE IDENTICAL EPITAPH:
"HERE I LIE IN A GARDEN MILD WAITING FOR MY WIFE AND CHILD"

THE BEGGAR'S MEMORIAL
Yunnan Sen, China
FOR 73 YEARS
HUN LIANG PLEADED FOR ALMS-
BUT BEFORE HIS DEATH HE
DIRECTED THAT THE COINS HE HAD
COLLECTED BE MELTED TO
ERECT A SOLID BRONZE
PAGODA - AS A MONUMENT
TO THE GENEROSITY OF HIS
BENEFACTORS!
HE HAD NOT SPENT A SINGLE
ONE OF THE COINS

PEPPER POT
TOMBSTONE
OF THE
PEPPER FAMILY
Stuttgart, Germany

THE MANGROVE TOMBSTONES OF ANGOLA
Portuguese Africa
A TREE IS BENT INTO A CIRCLE OVER EACH GRAVE TO PROVIDE A **HANDGRIP** SO THE **DEPARTED SOUL** CAN **RESIST** THE **PULL** OF THE **DEVIL**!

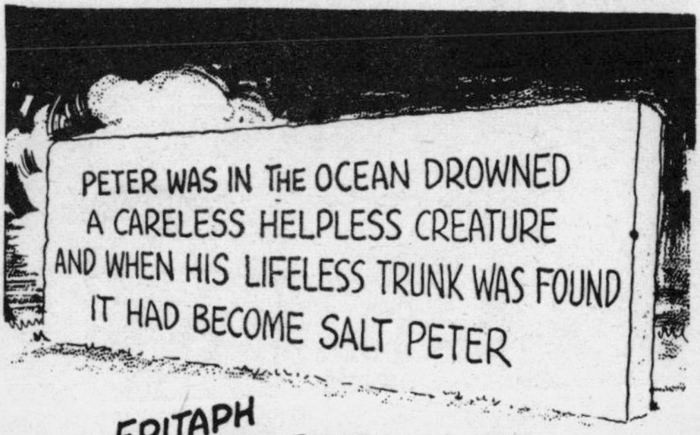
PETER WAS IN THE OCEAN DROWNED
A CARELESS HELPLESS CREATURE
AND WHEN HIS LIFELESS TRUNK WAS FOUND
IT HAD BECOME SALT PETER

EPITAPH OF PETER WILSON
Hasbro' Churchyard, England

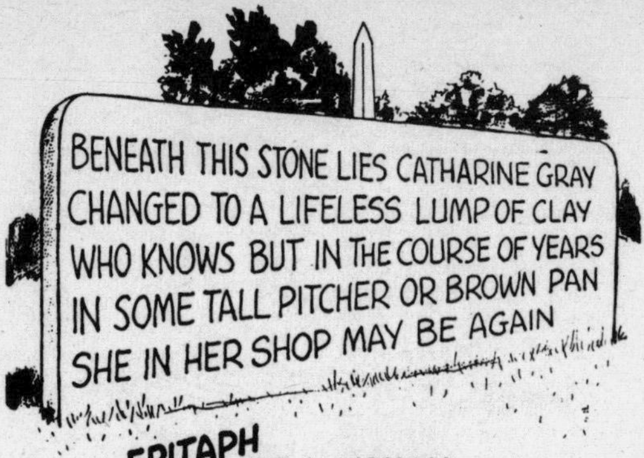
BENEATH THIS STONE LIES CATHARINE GRAY
CHANGED TO A LIFELESS LUMP OF CLAY
WHO KNOWS BUT IN THE COURSE OF YEARS
IN SOME TALL PITCHER OR BROWN PAN
SHE IN HER SHOP MAY BE AGAIN

EPITAPH OF A WOMAN
WHO OWNED A POTTERY SHOP
Chester, England

ELIZA SORROWING
REARS THIS MARBLE SLAB
TO HER DEAR JOHN
WHO DIED OF EATING CRAB

EPITAPH IN THE CHURCHYARD
AT GREENWICH, Eng.

HAND
OF
J.T. BANDY
NOV. 25, 1913

TOMBSTONE
in
cemetery
near
Roanoke,
Va.

THE OLD MAIDS WHO KEPT A DEAD HORSE IN THEIR PARLOR!

ANGELINA and BLOSSOM SWEAT
of Bedford, N.H.

WERE SO FOND OF THEIR HORSE THAT WHEN IT DIED THEY HAD IT STUFFED AND MOUNTED – ***AND DISPLAYED IT IN FULL HARNESS IN THEIR HOME FOR THE REMAINDER OF THEIR LIVES***

GRAVE OF SPITE
WILLIAM AND AGNES LOUDON of Pinner, Middlesex, Eng.
WERE ENTOMBED IN A TALL POINTED STRUCTURE ABOVE THE EARTH AS DIRECTED IN THEIR WILLS TO THWART THE CLAIMS OF HEIRS -ENGLISH LAW STATES THAT NO INHERITANCE CAN BE TOUCHED UNTIL THE BODY OF THE DECEDENT BE PLACED "UNDER GROUND"

THE TOMBS OF BUDDHIST PRIESTS

ARE EARTHEN JARS WHICH ARE LEFT STANDING IN ANY OPEN FIELD

WIDOW
SUSANNA BROWNSON
WAS BORN AUGUST 3,1699
AND DIED JUNE 12,1802
AGED 103 YEARS

GRAVESTONE OF A WOMAN WHO LIVED IN 3 CENTURIES

Landaff, N.H., Cemetery

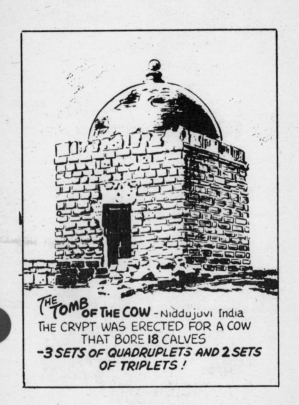

THE TOMB OF THE COW - Niddujuvi India
THE CRYPT WAS ERECTED FOR A COW THAT BORE 18 CALVES
-3 SETS OF QUADRUPLETS AND 2 SETS OF TRIPLETS!

JOHN BUCKHOUT
DIED...1785
AGE 103
LEAVING BEHIND
240
CHILDREN
AND
GRANDCHILDREN

GRAVESTONE in SLEEPY HOLLOW CEMETERY, New York

HE THAT GIVES AWAY ALL
BEFORE HE IS DEAD
LET THEM TAKE A HATCHET
AND KNOCK HIM ON YE HEAD

GRAVESTONE in Leominster Churchyard England

HERE LIES
A. TOOMB
BENEATH
A TOMB

GRAVE OF ANDREW TOOMB Scioto County, Ohio

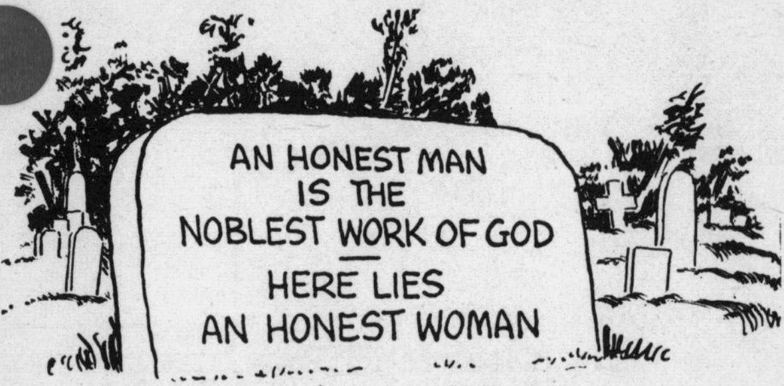
AN HONEST MAN
IS THE
NOBLEST WORK OF GOD
HERE LIES
AN HONEST WOMAN

GRAVESTONE in the Bottisham Churchyard
Cambridge, England

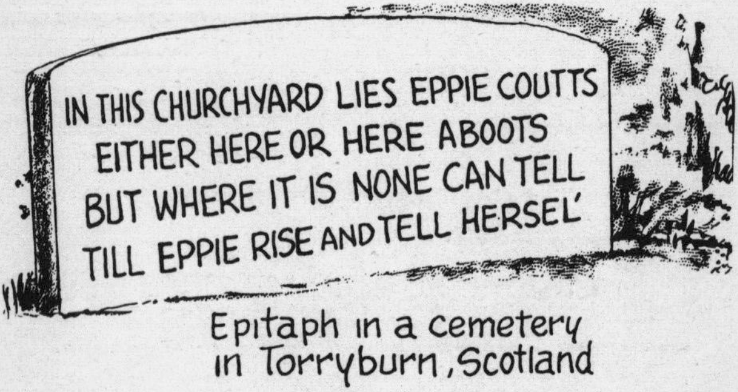
IN THIS CHURCHYARD LIES EPPIE COUTTS
EITHER HERE OR HERE ABOOTS
BUT WHERE IT IS NONE CAN TELL
TILL EPPIE RISE AND TELL HERSEL'

Epitaph in a cemetery
in Torryburn, Scotland

THE GRAVES OF THE GHOST RIDERS

HITCHING POSTS

ADORN THE GRAVES OF THE YAKUTS OF SIBERIA IN THE BELIEF THAT THE SOULS OF THE DEPARTED *NIGHTLY RIDE HORSEBACK THROUGH THE COUNTRYSIDE!*

THE
ARMENIANS
USE
LAMB-SHAPED TOMBSTONES!

THE LAMB BEING THE SYMBOL OF CHRIST

These Tombstones Are Forbidden in Soviet Armenia

MEMORIAL TO A PUMP

"THIS OLD PUMP NOW AT REST STANDS AS A MEMORIAL TO THOSE IT SERVED"

PLAQUE ON A PUMP PRESERVED IN CEMETERY AT OAK CREEK, WIS.

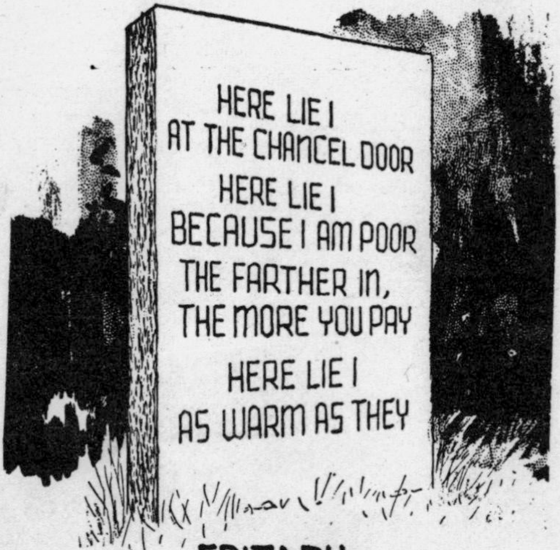
HERE LIE I
AT THE CHANCEL DOOR
HERE LIE I
BECAUSE I AM POOR
THE FARTHER IN,
THE MORE YOU PAY
HERE LIE I
AS WARM AS THEY

EPITAPH
in Kingsbridge Churchyard
Devon, England

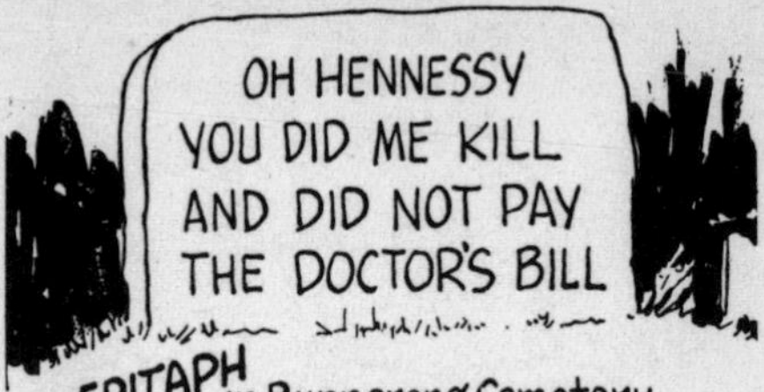
OH HENNESSY
YOU DID ME KILL
AND DID NOT PAY
THE DOCTOR'S BILL

EPITAPH in Bunnerong Cemetery
-Sydney, Australia

HERE LIES
F. K.
WHO LIVED
26 YRS AS A MAN
37 AS A HUSBAND

GRAVESTONE
IN JACKSONVILLE, Florida

HERE LIES
WILD BILL BRITT
RAN FOR SHERIFF IN '82
RAN FROM SHERIFF IN '83
BURIED IN '84

TOMBSTONE IN RUIDOSO, N. Mexico

GRAVESTONE
IN MEMPHIS, Tenn.

GRAVESTONE
IN JACKSONVILLE, Fla.

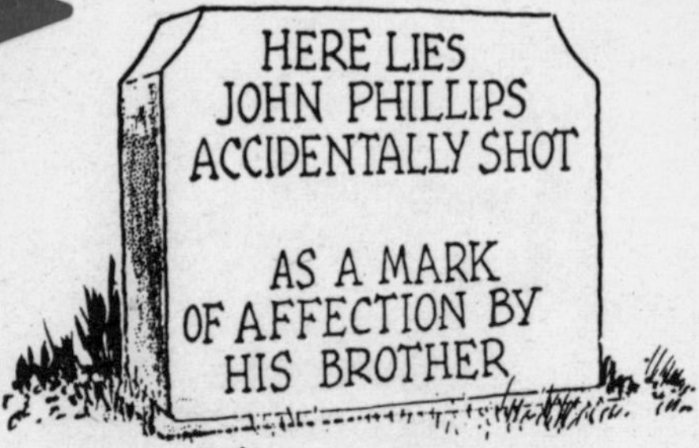
HERE LIES
JOHN PHILLIPS
ACCIDENTALLY SHOT

AS A MARK
OF AFFECTION BY
HIS BROTHER

EPITAPH IN A CEMETERY
Bath, Maine

DOCTOR
FRED ROBERTS
1875 - 1931
OFFICE UPSTAIRS

PINE LOG CEMETERY
Brookland, Ark.

HERE LIES A MAN
WHO FIRST DID DYE
WHEN HE WAS 24
BUT NOW HE'S GONE
AND CERTAIN 'TIS
HE'LL NOT DYE
ANYMORE

TOMBSTONE OF A DYER
St. Nicholas Churchyard
Yarmouth, England

GOOD
NIGHT
NICHOLAS

EPITAPH ON THE
GRAVE OF KNIGHT
NICHOLAS MARTIN
in Puddletown
Churchyard,
England

THE MEMORIAL TO THE "DUNBAR"
A SAILING SHIP THAT WENT DOWN NEAR Sydney, Australia, in 1857 WITH A LOSS OF 121 MEN
DISPLAYS THE VESSEL'S OWN ANCHOR

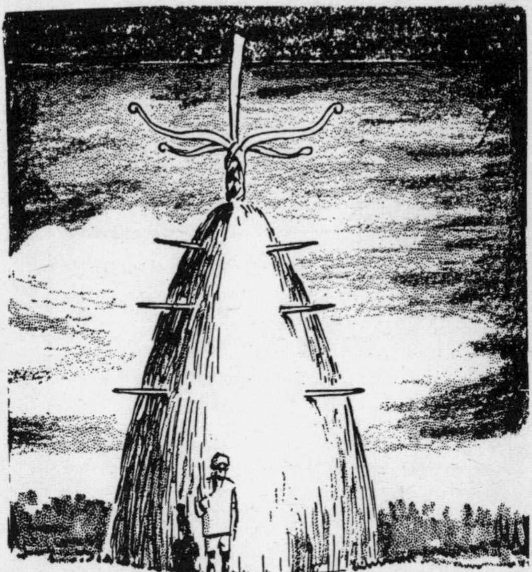

GRAVES of the **KACHIN TRIBE** - Burma
ARE 3 TIMES AS BIG AS THEIR HOUSES!
THEY BELIEVE THE SOUL EXPANDS AFTER DEATH ***SO THEY BUILD IT A HUT 20 FEET HIGH***

GOEMBEL
JOHN E.
1867 - 1946
"THE DEFENSE RESTS"

TOMBSTONE
OF AN ATTORNEY
Willwood Cemetery
Rockford, Ill.

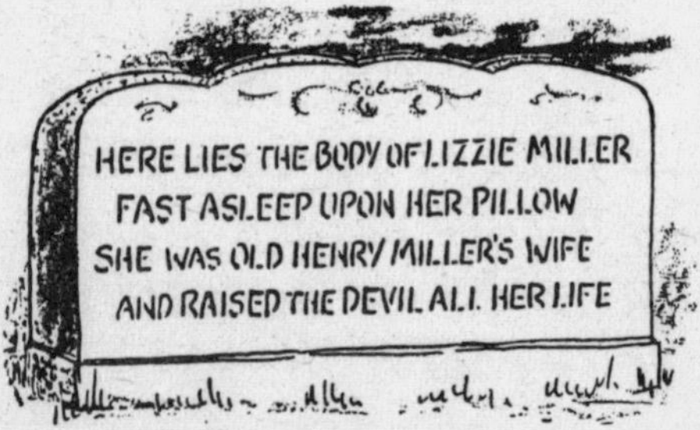
HERE LIES THE BODY OF LIZZIE MILLER
FAST ASLEEP UPON HER PILLOW
SHE WAS OLD HENRY MILLER'S WIFE
AND RAISED THE DEVIL ALL HER LIFE

TOMBSTONE IN Alexandria, Va.

YANG TSEN HSING Governor General of Sinkiang

ATTEMPTED TO OUTWIT THE ANGEL OF DEATH BY CONSTRUCTING A MAGNIFICENT TOMB THEN ORDERING A COOLIE TO ASSUME HIS NAME - YANG TSEN HSING - WHEREUPON HE HAD THE COOLIE KILLED AND BURIED IN THE TOMB DESTINED FOR HIMSELF

ABNER COLUMBUS SHARPE
SEPT. 24, 1857-MAR. 25, 1927
HE WAS "A DEMOCRAT"

TOMBSTONE IN Statesville Cemetery, N.C.

THE MONUMENT in Thorshavn, Denmark, TO DR. NIELS FINSEN

DISCOVERER OF THE VALUE OF SUNLIGHT IN TREATING SKIN DISEASES, WAS BUILT AROUND A HUGE ROCK INTO WHICH ***AS A YOUNG BOY HE HAD CHISELED HIS OWN NAME***

-1904-

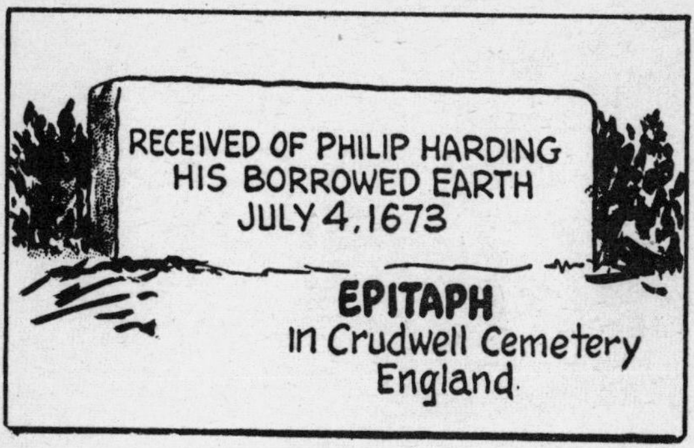
RECEIVED OF PHILIP HARDING
HIS BORROWED EARTH
JULY 4, 1673

EPITAPH
in Crudwell Cemetery
England

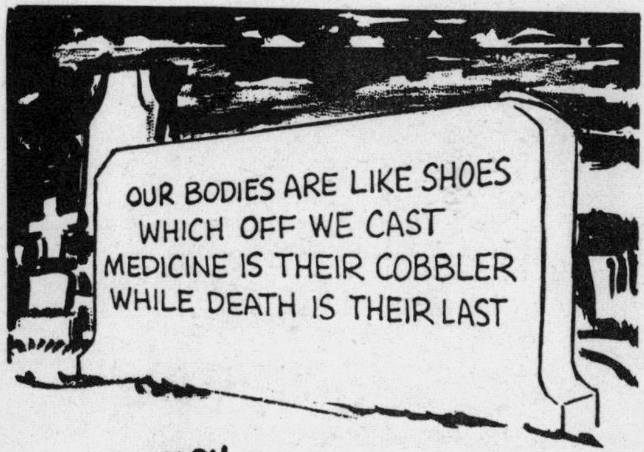
OUR BODIES ARE LIKE SHOES
WHICH OFF WE CAST
MEDICINE IS THEIR COBBLER
WHILE DEATH IS THEIR LAST

EPITAPH
in Cirencester Cemetery
England

SALOON SIGN IN CEMETERY, Hawesville, Ky.
JOE ALDRIGE OWNED THE LOG CABIN SALOON
WHEN HE DIED HE REQUESTED HIS CABIN BE USED
AS A MONUMENT TO HIS MEMORY.

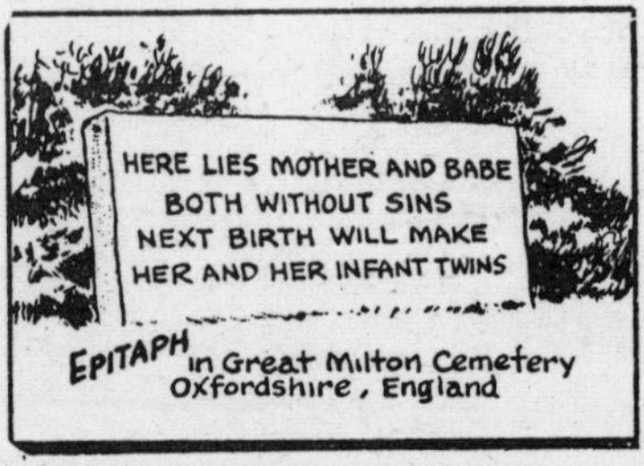
HERE LIES MOTHER AND BABE
BOTH WITHOUT SINS
NEXT BIRTH WILL MAKE
HER AND HER INFANT TWINS
EPITAPH in Great Milton Cemetery
Oxfordshire, England

TOMBSTONES ARE ERECTED IN INDO-CHINA OVER THE GRAVES OF **WILD TIGERS!**
NATIVES HOPE TO ESCAPE THE VENGEANCE OF THE SLAIN ANIMAL'S SPIRIT

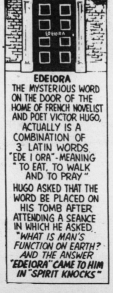

EDEIORA
THE MYSTERIOUS WORD ON THE DOOR OF THE HOME OF FRENCH NOVELIST AND POET VICTOR HUGO, ACTUALLY IS A COMBINATION OF 3 LATIN WORDS. "EDE I ORA" - MEANING " TO EAT, TO WALK AND TO PRAY "
HUGO ASKED THAT THE WORD BE PLACED ON HIS TOMB AFTER ATTENDING A SEANCE IN WHICH HE ASKED. *"WHAT IS MAN'S FUNCTION ON EARTH?* *AND THE ANSWER* ***"EDEIORA" CAME TO HIM IN "SPIRIT KNOCKS"***

JOSEF STOKLAS - gravedigger of Heiligenblut, Jugoslavia VOWED TO DIG 1,000 GRAVES - AND DID - BUT WAS HIMSELF BURIED IN HIS 1,000th GRAVE! HE DROPPED DEAD AS HE SHOVELED THE LAST SPADEFUL OF EARTH

JOSEPH BAKER
IS **BURIED *STANDING UP***
INSIDE A STONE PYRAMID ON A
MOUNTAIN SIDE
Near Winchester, Va

A CITY GATE
in Ayassoluk, Turkey,
BUILT BY THE GREEKS 1,600
YEARS AGO, WAS CONSTRUCTED
OUT OF TOMBSTONES
AND COFFIN LIDS

RODERIQUE
a French sailor
WHOSE SWEETHEART
DIED IN TAHITI, HAD
HER TOMB TATTOOED
OVER HIS HEART

THE TOMB OF DOOM!

THE MAUSOLEUM OF EMPEROR TU DUC
of Annam, Indochina
WAS BUILT BY 2,500 LABORERS WHO TOILED FOR 30 YEARS -- AND THEN WERE BEHEADED TO KEEP SECRET *THE EXACT LOCATION OF HIS BODY!*

HEAD STONES OF LEAH KREIDER - AND HER 10 CHILDREN —— ALL IN A ROW - Lancaster, Pa.
EACH OF HER 10 CHILDREN DIED THE DAY THEY WERE BORN

THE JAPANESE NUMBER 13
RESEMBLES A TOMBSTONE

THREE-FAMILY GRAVESTONE
Westminster Cemetery, Philadelphia

THE BEER BOTTLE MONUMENT
A NATIVE OF TONGATABU ISLAND IN THE SOUTH PACIFIC WAS SO PROUD OF HIS BEER BOTTLE COLLECTION THAT IT WAS USED TO MARK HIS GRAVE

THIS STONE WAS RAISED BY SARA'S LORD
NOT SARA'S VIRTUES TO RECORD
FOR THEY ARE KNOWN TO ALL THE TOWN
THIS STONE WAS RAISED TO KEEP HER DOWN

EPITAPH
in Kilmory Churchyard -Scotland

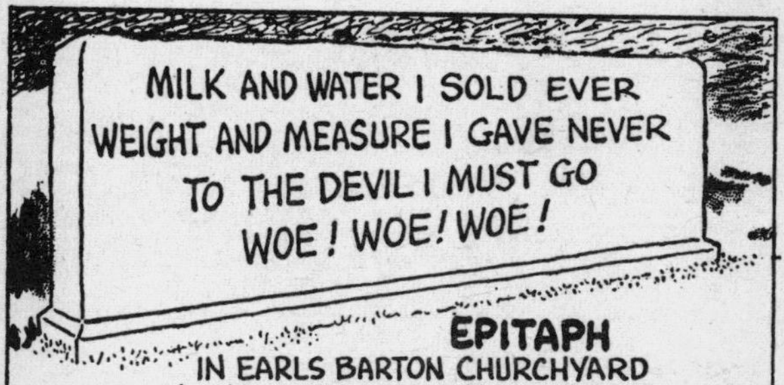
MILK AND WATER I SOLD EVER
WEIGHT AND MEASURE I GAVE NEVER
TO THE DEVIL I MUST GO
WOE! WOE! WOE!

EPITAPH
IN EARLS BARTON CHURCHYARD
Northamptonshire, England

THE TOMBS of Haitian peasants ARE OFTEN RESPLENDENT STRUCTURES *EVEN THOUGH THEY MAY HAVE LIVED ALL THEIR LIVES IN WRETCHED HUTS*

COFFIN

CONTAINING THE BODY OF HENRY TRIGGS HAS BEEN STORED UPON THE ROOF OF HIS COTTAGE FOR THE LAST 225 YEARS -

SO THAT HE MIGHT BE AT HOME ON THE DAY OF RESURRECTION!

Stevenage,
England

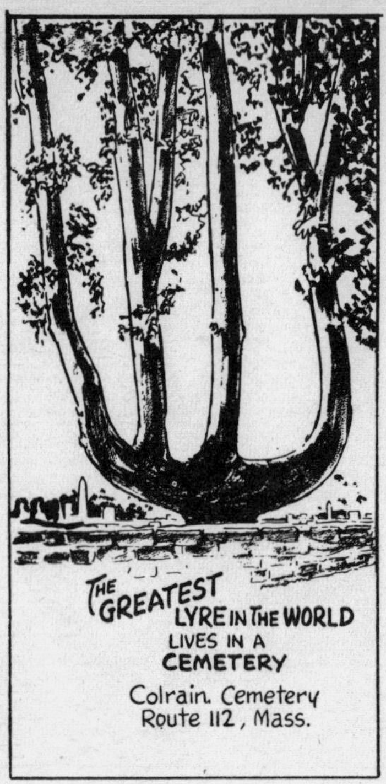

THE GREATEST LYRE IN THE WORLD LIVES IN A CEMETERY

Colrain. Cemetery
Route 112, Mass.

SKELETON CARVED ON THE TOMB OF JOHN SHAWE—TO DEPICT HIM AS HE EXPECTED TO LOOK **10 YEARS AFTER DEATH**
-in the Church of Rivington, England

GREEN BEAN
BORN
APR 11 - 1841
DIED
MAR 27 - 1892
AGED
50 YRS - 11 MS. - 16 D

TOMBSTONE IN THE BEAN FAMILY CEMETERY near Mitchell, Mo.

I PROMISE
NEVER TO
MARRY
AGAIN
JACK

EVERGREEN CEMETERY
Jacksonville, Florida